Blended Learning and Online Tutoring

Blended Learning and Online Tutoring

A Good Practice Guide

JANET MACDONALD

GOWER

Aldershot
Hampshire GU11 3HR
England

Gower Publishing Company
Suite 420
101 Cherry Street
Burlington, VT 05401-4405
USA

Janet Macdonald has asserted her moral right under the Copyright, Designs and Patents Act, 1988, to be identified as the author of this work.

British Library Cataloguing in Publication Data
Macdonald, Janet
    Blended learning and online tutoring: a good practice
    guide
    1. Blended learning 2. Distance education 3. Telecommunication
    I. Title
    371.3'58

ISBN: 0 566 08659 X

Library of Congress Cataloging-in-Publication Data
Macdonald, Janet, 1950–
    Blended learning and online tutoring: a good practice guide / by Janet Macdonald.
      p. cm.
    ISBN 0-566-08659-X
    1.Blended learning. 2. Blended learning--Case studies. 3. Education, Higher--
Computer-assisted instruction. 4. Internet in higher education. I. Title

  LB1028.5.M124 2005
  378.1'734--dc22

                                                                  2005030373

Printed and bound in Great Britain by TJ International Ltd, Padstow, Cornwall.

CONTENTS

ACKNOWLEDGEMENTS

I would like to thank Peter Syme, Director of the Open University (OU) in Scotland, and many other colleagues at the OU, both in Scotland and in other parts of the UK, who contributed moral support, and who read parts of the script or gave me helpful comments.

I'm indebted to the many OU tutors who supplied the 'bright ideas' which feature throughout this book, and who also participated in the SOLACE project. Many OU students have also contributed their perspectives on using a computer for study.

I am particularly grateful to Sylvia Warnecke and the Languages, Maths and Computing tutors at the Open University in Scotland, who have contributed greatly to my understanding of differences in approaches to supporting students in their three very different disciplines, and to good practice guidelines in using synchronous tools, through a project on synchronous tuition in which we were recently engaged.

I was delighted to hear from so many contributors to the blended learning survey, and have learnt much from those who so kindly sent me case studies. My particular thanks go to Sonja Cameron for her contribution in working with me in the analysis of the data.

I am grateful to Anne Gaskell and co-authors of the Supporting Students by Telephone toolkit, since many of the good practice guidelines for telephone tuition which they have collected apply equally well to other synchronous tools.

I am grateful to the Scottish Higher Education Funding Council, and also to the Centre for Research in Education and Educational Technology, Open University UK, for funding two projects described in this book.

Finally, my family, Murdo, Ewan and Kirsten, have patiently put up with my book writing and mental absences over the past year, and they have my love and thanks.

CHAPTER 1

INTRODUCTION

The word 'blended' is not particularly scientific, or even academic. In fact, you might feel that it sounds rather more like an entry from a recipe book. At the same time, it is currently widely in use by practitioners in both academic and commercial sectors, and I believe it has some good common-sense value in bringing to the fore the wide variety and richness of situations in which learning takes place. It can encourage us to stop and think about the whole context of teaching and learning, so that we remember the human element in tutorials, or perhaps incidents such as chance meetings in the corridor, as critical parts of the package alongside any technology-mediated intervention with a group.

With changes in student demography, increasingly large classes, and a growth in part-time study, many course developers and tutors are turning to online media for teaching and learning. However, challenges and tensions arise where institutions are also concerned with widening access and retention. Very often tutors find that online approaches do not work quite as the books say they should. There are questions to address. Is online learning appropriate for all my students; does it represent a cost-effective use of the tutor's time; are we supporting our students, or abandoning them? In this chapter I set out some of the issues, then outline what the book contains and who I think might be interested in reading it.

DISTANCE TECHNOLOGIES: POTENTIAL AND PITFALLS

Distance technologies have opened up new potential in higher education, and the literature is full of enthusiastic predictions. For example, networks offer scope for new ways to access and combine information using the limitless resources of the Web. Students at a distance, or separated from their peers for other reasons, no longer need to work in isolation but can join other learners in an electronically supported community. These developments offer the possibilities to develop greater self-direction in learners and to move away from teacher-directed approaches to teaching and learning. Instead of receiving information or knowledge from the teacher, students can be encouraged to seek out information for themselves and to develop their understanding by reflecting on course concepts with their peers. In these new approaches, there is a greater importance attached to understanding, rather than simply memorising and reproducing facts.

These are optimistic horizons, and conjure up a halcyon view of networked study. At the same time, we know that not all students like learning exclusively online, or perhaps the experience was not quite what they expected. They may not participate fully and can even vote with their feet. There are serious health warnings in terms of student retention on some courses which wholeheartedly embrace online learning.

It is time we looked at good practice in online tutoring in the context of what we know about our students, what else we do with them, how we support them, and what other opportunities they have for learning from each other. It makes sense: after all, the experience of studying online while sitting in a computer lab, with the possibility of exchanging ideas or the odd joke with fellow students sitting next to you will be very different to that of students who are studying at home, with only a computer for company.

BLENDED LEARNING AND BLENDED TEACHING STRATEGIES

Blended learning is something of a hot topic nowadays, but like the term 'e-learning', everyone has a different understanding of what it means. Early references to blended learning come from industry and workplace learning, although recently it has become more widely adopted in higher education (HE) institutions. The term is commonly associated with the introduction of online media into a course or programme, while at the same time recognising that there is merit in retaining face-to-face contact and other traditional approaches to supporting students. It is also used where asynchronous media such as email or conferencing are deployed in conjunction with synchronous technologies, commonly text chat or audio.

Blended learning seems to have arisen from a general sense of disillusionment with the stand-alone adoption of online media. Many people felt that the promise of online media was somehow unfulfilled. In fact, Mason (2002) comments: '... the earlier e-learning adopters have come full circle in rejecting an "either or" view of learning online versus face-to-face ... so called blended solutions often offer the most satisfactory outcomes'. Laurillard (2002) suggests that a balance of media is essential to make learning and teaching effective, and the information and communications technology (ICT) element is unlikely to contribute to more than 50 per cent of the total strategy.

My view is that we should set aside discussions on the appropriate blend of media and plan for the effective support of student learning, whether for individuals or groups, in both formal and informal ways. While automated learner support makes a valuable contribution, for example through online quizzes or simulations, I believe the choice of appropriate tutor-mediated support is central to blended learning. In fact, blended learning can and should enhance responsiveness to student needs by an informed choice or intervention strategy, whether that is online or face to face.

I intend to develop a more detailed description of the characteristics of blended learning later in this book, but I should point out that there has already been much useful and relevant work in the field, from people who have not used the term blended learning, and yet refer to the same or very similar concepts. For example, papers on online or networked learning very often refer incidentally to the use of synchronous face-to-face or telephone tuition sessions, alongside the use of online asynchronous learning.

> *Networked learning in undergraduate education in the UK is rarely – probably never – used without some kind of opportunities for face-to-face interaction. The tendency is to find ways of blending CMC [computer-mediated communication] with more traditional forms of activity, seeking to get the best from a mix of different methods.* (Goodyear et al., 2005)

Another term with similar connotations is 'distributed learning', meaning a convergence of traditional distance and on-campus education. In fact, one of the most fascinating aspects of blended strategies is this convergence of interests between traditional campus-based learning, and open and distance learning. With the introduction of online media and with changing student markets and a greater emphasis on lifelong learning, the two contexts are not as far apart as they once were. However, access issues in a campus-based environment are likely to be very different to those faced by distance students.

For distance institutions such as the Open University (UK) where I work, or for campus-based institutions with distance students, the motivation for adopting blended strategies may hinge on the choice of both synchronous and asynchronous alternatives to face-to-face tutorials as a strategy to accommodate the varying geographical or temporal challenges faced by our students. With the widespread use of online media in the population at large, and the exciting educational opportunities that they offer, we are looking at new ways of supporting students and reassessing what we do currently. On the other hand, for campus-based staff whose students are readily available for face-to-face intervention, the emphasis may be on supplementing class contact time and providing enhanced opportunities for supporting a wide diversity of student needs. I believe that as academic communities we have much to learn from each other.

WHAT THIS BOOK CONTAINS

Part I of this book concentrates on current practice in blended learning, in both campus-based and distance institutions. In Chapters 2 and 3, I discuss a study of Open University tutors' strategies for supporting students, and their reflections on what they value in their contact with students. They describe a variety of approaches to supporting students, for a wide range of reasons, and their reflections underline the fact that no single intervention strategy using one medium could possibly support all students effectively.

Chapters 4 and 5 describe a survey of current practice in blended learning in 50 universities and colleges, primarily in Europe and Australasia. The adoption of blended learning and the use of a variety of technologies are influenced by various pragmatic and pedagogic concerns, illustrated here with extracts from those who contributed to the survey.

Part II describes practical ways of using online tools for supporting students in both asynchronous and synchronous environments. Online conferences can be used for tutor-mediated support in a variety of ways. The purpose of the conference and its membership have implications for the extent of student participation, the roles of the conference moderator, and the time needed to support students. Chapters 6 and 7 cover best practice in the use of online asynchronous media.

The deployment of synchronous time with students is probably one of the most difficult issues to resolve when designing a blended teaching strategy. In campus-based environments, synchronous intervention has long been associated with the delivery of content, although in many cases other elements of student support have come into play. The move to adopt new patterns of content delivery and support demands a critical appraisal of how synchronous elements can best contribute to the support of students. This is particularly important for distance students, where synchronous meetings may be problematic. Although Chapters 8 and 9 concentrate on the use of synchronous media, there are implications for new ways in which face-to-face sessions might also be used.

Part III covers approaches to learning development for students who will study online as part of a blended course. Very often such courses demand a degree of self-direction and motivation which may be unfamiliar to those who were previously used to traditional models of education. Chapter 10 describes student perspectives, and Chapter 11 concentrates on coherent course design, which ensures that the various learning activities and interventions are aligned with course learning objectives and authentic assessment design. Finally, in Chapters 12 to 14, I discuss three interrelated areas in the development of competent blended learners: e-investigating, e-writing and e-collaborating, and illustrate this with a variety of practical designs for developing competence and self-direction through course activities and assessment.

I have emphasised the central role of the tutor in a blended strategy. If tutors are to be deployed in new roles, then they need appropriate training and professional development. Chapter 15 describes tutors' perspectives on blended learning, and the practical constraints facing staff developers. It goes on to discuss a variety of strategies that have been used to provide formal and informal approaches to staff development.

WHO THIS BOOK IS FOR

I have written this book for practitioners who are contemplating blended learning and online tutoring for their course, or staff developers who wish to encourage others. I hope it is a practical book. I have tried to steer away from armfuls of references to learned articles, but at the same time have been anxious to base my observations on the excellent work on student learning which has been undertaken by many of my colleagues.

I may be based in a distance-learning university, but remain firmly convinced of the ground which we have in common with campus institutions. I hope this book will find application and a readership in both camps.

A PERSONAL REFLECTION

I have lived with this book for the last year. It has been a formative experience for me, and has led me to think long and hard about the relationship between asynchronous and synchronous events, and the way in which I myself work or study.

In the process of writing this book I began to realise how much the process of writing is divided between a synchronous element, as I put 'pen to paper', and an asynchronous element, as I revised subsequent drafts and rethought ways of expressing concepts and explaining ideas at odd times of the day or night.

When I was a research student and working some 300 miles from my supervisors on campus, I remember well how much I valued our monthly telephone conversations. For routine communication and even data collection on asynchronous conferencing, there was no problem with my geographical location. However, after a few weeks of asynchronous working, my progress slowed to a standstill because I felt so isolated and alone. A telephone conversation was enough to get me started again: it worked like a tonic, every time.

In my working life at the Open University, often in touch with colleagues who are geographically remote, it has made me think about the value and centrality of the personal element in the working environment, and the importance of going out of my way to make opportunities to meet people face to face, or over the telephone, since we otherwise rely so heavily on asynchronous contact through email, with all its capacity for misunderstandings.

A blend of the two just makes life a bit more bearable.

RESOURCES

Goodyear, P., Jones, C., Asensio, M., Hodgson, V. and Steeples, C. (2005) 'Networked learning in higher education: students' expectations and experiences'. *Higher Education,* **50** (3), pp. 473–508.

Laurillard, D. (2002) *Rethinking University Teaching. A conversational framework for the effective use of learning technologies* (London, Routledge, second edition).

Mason, R. (2002) *E-learning: What have we learnt? Improving student learning using learning technology* (Proceedings of the 2001 9th International Student Learning Symposium), pp. 27–34.

PART I

APPROACHES TO BLENDED LEARNING

CHAPTER 2

TUTOR-MEDIATED SUPPORT:
REFLECTING ON PRESENT PRACTICE

The use of online media in both distance and campus-based environments offers opportunities for supporting learners which were not previously available. We all suffer from a flood of communication through email with both fellow staff and students. Many staff will use a website to post lecture notes or slide presentations. At the same time, we continue to run lectures, face-to-face tutorials or seminars as we have always done. How effective are these strategies, and where should we be expending most effort? What represents cost-effective use of the tutor's time, and what constitutes an acceptable level of duplication?

One way to begin thinking about these questions is to reflect on present practice. The aim of this chapter is to describe an exercise in reflective practice in which we have recently been engaged at the Open University (UK), and the parallels we have been able to draw with a campus-based context. I hope this will give you the opportunity to think about what you do now, in supporting your own students' learning.

THE SOLACE PROJECT

SOLACE (Supporting Open Learners in A Changing Environment) was an action research project which aimed to enhance our understanding of current practice, aims and objectives in tutor-mediated support, and the potential of available and developing technologies to meet these challenges. We wanted to find out what tutors do now, and how they make use of online media, alongside other ways of supporting their students. We did this by asking 40 tutors from all faculties to share with their peers their experiences of supporting students. Since our tutors may be geographically widely distributed, we used an asynchronous computer conference as a platform for their shared reflection.

In order to create a structure for this reflective practice and to ensure that they were all working to the same aims and objectives, we asked them to contribute logs of their activities in supporting students. We decided to concentrate on three key points of the course presentation: the course start, mid-course and course end. Each participant was randomly allocated a week in which to record their activity, and having completed their week's recording they were asked to upload it to the computer conference, and to discuss their experiences with fellow tutors. The observations I make here and in the next chapter are based on an analysis of data from 80 logs, and the transcripts of some 600 conference messages.

I have included two completed logs, so that you can see how two tutors approached the task. The log provided space for tutors to record the number of contacts they had with students, the medium used and the range of functions which these contacts involved. It includes not only formal contacts which are foreseeable and form part of scheduled duties, but also informal contacts, many of them taking place with individual students. You will see that we have distinguished between 'proactive' contact, being that initiated by the tutor, and 'reactive', being that initiated by the students themselves. We also asked for an estimate of how many students were reached by each intervention, in order to get a measure of the relative attendance. The logs shown in Tables 2.1 and 2.2 are from different courses: a second level history course (group A); a third level course in health and social care (group B).

Table 2.1   SOLACE log showing a week's activities with tutorial group A

Course logged	A220	Week beginning	21 June	
No. students	26	SOLACE ID	A1	

	Contact with group				
	Tel. conf.	Postal mailing	F-to-F tutorial	Comp conf. msg.	Email to list
No. contacts			1		
No. students reached			8		
Nature of intervention					
Administrative (introduction/dates/agendas/hols)			X		
Encouragement/lifestyle related			X		
Reinforcing concepts/course content (explanations/egs/alternative perspectives)			X		
Assignment prep			X		
Process of study (critical thinking/writing appropriately/use of evidence)					
Other					

	Contact with individuals				
	Tel.	Email	Letter	Assignment feedback	Other (e.g. extra session)
No. proactive contacts					
No. reactive contacts	7	9	1		
Nature of intervention					
Administrative (introduction/dates/agendas/hols)	X	X	X		
Encouragement/lifestyle related	X	X			
Reinforcing concepts/course content (explanations/egs/alternative perspectives)		X	X		
Assignment prep		X	X		
Process of study (critical thinking/writing appropriately/use of evidence)					
Other					

Additional tutorial in Aberdeen, to meet this year's distribution of students .... Telephone – RAF serviceman whose duties necessitate assignment extensions. Letter – student who missed Aberdeen tutorial through sudden illness. One of three emails – follow up to Aberdeen tutorial for one student still having difficulties with the material. Some dozen contacts by telephone and email re worries over obscurity in impending assignment. ...

Pre-summer contacts – re assignments; my movements in July/August (holiday then summer school); extensions to assignment submission dates. Students have settled down into e-mail users and phone-users, and I respond accordingly. Probably the two instances of e-mail fitting the bill are 1) dealing (a little briskly) with one student who has already had a fair ration of telephone and tutorial time in respect of paraphrasing the next assignment – it served to put on record limits beyond which he shouldn't stray. 2) dealing with the unexpected surge in enquiries (above) as to the [wording of assignment]. ... there's the usual sense of taking stock midway through the year and making provision for loss of contact or more desultory contact during July and August.

Table 2.2   SOLACE log showing a week's activities with tutorial group B

Course logged	K301	Week beginning	30 Aug			
No. students	13	SOLACE ID	K3			

	Contact with tutorial group				
	Tel. conf.	Postal mailing	F-to-F tutorial	Comp conf. msg.	Email to list
No. contacts		1	1		
No. students reached		3	9		
Nature of intervention					
Administrative *(introduction/dates/agendas/hols)*		X	X		
Encouragement/lifestyle related		X	X		
Reinforcing concepts/course content *(explanations/egs/alternative perspectives)*		X	X		
Assignment prep		X	X		
Process of study *(critical thinking/writing appropriately/use of evidence)*		X	X		
Other					

	Contact with individuals				
	Tel.	Email	Letter	Assignment feedback	Other (e.g. special session)
No. proactive contacts					
No. reactive contacts		2		11	1
Nature of intervention					
Administrative *(introduction/dates/agendas/hols)*		X		X	X
Encouragement/lifestyle related		X		X	X
Reinforcing concepts/course content *(explanations/egs/alternative perspectives)*				X	
Assignment prep		X		X	
Process of study *(critical thinking/writing appropriately/use of evidence)*		X		X	
Other					X

This is a busy and anxious time for the students [and me!]. They have just completed the last assignment and have their examinable component due 9th October. There is a full-day compulsory workshop on the 13th September and students often see this as an interruption in their revision and examinable component writing. The workshop is from 10am – 4pm and students from all 3 groups choose to attend either the Edinburgh or the Glasgow workshop.

I have had quite a high attendance at the tutorials this year – and I sent out tutorial notes, usually by e-mail attachment, to those who do not attend. I think this high attendance has cut down the need for telephone calls – proactive and reactive. Overall there has been a drop in phone calls and an increase in the use of e-mails for quick questions/answers, extension requests and so on since I started as a tutor, 12 years ago.

In parallel with this exercise, we extended the study to include three courses at the University of Glasgow, Scotland, so that we might try out the log in a campus-based environment (Macdonald and McAteer, 2003). We asked tutors at Glasgow University, which is a traditional campus-based institution, to concentrate on the support of learning, and to omit lectures, or written course materials, as they belong to learning content. At the same time, we recognised that in many campus-based institutions there will often be some overlap between the two, and the tutor is responsible for content delivery as well as tutorial support. I will comment later in this chapter on the similarities and differences between the two contexts.

BLENDING SUPPORT STRATEGIES

We discovered that the tutors were using a range of both online technologies and more conventional methods to support their students. Their current practice appeared to be the result of a gradual evolution over time, partly as a result of experience with the success or failure of particular strategies in the past.

The logs illustrated formal contact with groups of students, in addition to a wide range of informal contacts with individuals. The number of interactions waxed and waned from week to week in response to major events such as course start-up, tutorials or assignment deadlines. Some contacts were initiated by the tutor, and others by the students themselves.

Most contacts involved a range of the purposes listed here, often, for example, combining help with course concepts together with study skills and encouragement. The next two sections outline the patterns of support to the group and to individual students, which the tutors described in their logs. I hope it will give you the opportunity to compare their experiences with your own.

SUPPORTING THE GROUP

Face-to-face tutorials were widely in use for tuition to the group, as were online conferences or email to the group. In addition, some tutors were using telephone conferences as an alternative for students unable to attend face-to-face tutorials, or snail mail for groups who did not have email.

There were various reasons for the adoption of online support. Access issues, and falling attendance for other reasons, pose significant challenges to the effectiveness of face-to-face tutorials at the Open University (UK). In response, many faculties have adopted online media, and particularly computer conferencing, to provide an alternative means of tuition and support to learners. In some courses, online conferencing is employed effectively as a replacement for face-to-face tutorials, with online activities forming an integral part of the course, either throughout, or at particular points in the course.

> *Few have participated in the [computer] conference yet, but it is early days, and part of [assignment one] is to find my name in the conference and send me a message, which about half of them have managed so far.* (Maths tutor)

> *... asynchronous tutorials run over a week ... and they usually work well.* (Business school tutor)

More commonly, computer conferences were used as an adjunct to face-to-face tutorials. Such conferences might include recommendations to further reading, notices about forthcoming course events, or timely reminders, hints and tips for effective study.

> *Used [computer] conference to forward agenda for tutorial ... 15 students read this – and to inform students that the assignment has been marked and returned to the system – 10 students read this.* (Business school tutor)

> *I sent a message to our tutor group conference ... encouraging them to tackle the [final assignment] and to exchange ideas, questions and progress in our conference ...* (Technology tutor)

SUPPORTING THE INDIVIDUAL STUDENT

Formal contact with individual students took place through written feedback on assignments. In fact, this contact is central to the support of learners at the Open University (UK), where correspondence tuition is the only form of tuition that all students receive.

In addition to this formal contact, there were many contacts on an informal level. Most of these combined simple administrative enquiries with more complex needs for encouragement and help with assignment preparation. Tutors viewed these contacts as an important part of supporting learning:

a valued opportunity to keep up with individual student progress, and to identify students with particular needs for support.

While email was widely in use, tutors also made use of snail mail and the telephone.

> *... I had my first tutorial yesterday and there were lots of queries in the run-up to that ... Students were getting in touch to let me know whether or not they were attending – and how they were doing in general ...* (Languages tutor)

> *Students who have email tend to email me regularly. I think they feel more comfortable with email, than phoning when it might be inconvenient. It also means I can give a more considered response than is sometimes possible when students want an instant response to the phone query ...* (Humanities tutor)

Respondents describe email as in use for many of the contacts previously undertaken by snail mail, and some of the contacts undertaken by phone. It is perceived as a way of extending tutorial support beyond traditional real-time tutorials or assignment feedback.

Many tutors report more continuous contact from students than they had experienced before the widespread use of email. The use of email has been particularly significant in this context because it makes tutors more available to students than they have ever been before. This may signal pressure from some students for 'just in time' assistance, demanding more individual attention than they had previously enjoyed.

> *I notice that many of those with email will use it to supplement tutorial time with me, rather than have dialogue with peers.* (Education tutor)

In fact, we found that the tutors received around three times as many emails from students as they initiated, and roughly twice as many phone calls. Of course, any comparison between media in terms of numbers of contacts is bound to be a crude measure. After all, the number of emails or computer conference messages which you need to achieve a particular purpose may be considerably in excess of the number of phone calls, or meetings in the corridor, to achieve the same purpose. One synchronous intervention can range over a variety of subjects, in response to the tutor's probing and the student's response. In contrast, email exchanges can become an endless stream of communication, as the initial problem is identified and refined, and more complex and related issues emerge. For this reason alone, with increasing use of email, an increase in the number of contacts between tutors and individual students looks inevitable.

CONVERGENCE OF CAMPUS-BASED AND DISTANCE CONTEXTS

If you work in a campus-based institution, you might be wondering how much of this is of relevance to your own situation. My involvement in the SOLACE project, and in particular our work with Glasgow University, made me realise how much we have in common. In fact, there has been a convergence of interest from both campus-based and ODL (Open and Distance Learning) contexts in the concept of blended learning and teaching strategies.

However, I believe that the acceptability and feasibility of particular blended tuition strategies will depend on the overall teaching environment, the curriculum design and the availability of alternatives. In particular, access issues in a campus-based environment are likely to be very different from those faced by distance students. On some campuses, students may be readily available for face-to-face intervention, and so other synchronous options may be less relevant and understandably less attractive for both staff and students. For example, at Glasgow University we found that campus-based tutors regularly met their students face to face, and would not expect to use the telephone for tuition. On the other hand, for students who, by virtue of geographical or temporal isolation or high student:staff ratios, would otherwise be studying on their own, online or telephone tuition can be a lifeline. While asynchronous learning through computer conferencing is in use in both distance- and campus-based contexts, it may have greater significance for those students who have little or no alternative.

The role of informal exchanges is emerging as an important component of student learning, and is something which probably just 'happens' on campus, as these opportunities present themselves in walks to lectures, or meetings over coffee. While in both campus and distance environments email is regularly in use, other opportunities for informal exchange for distance students need to be rather more carefully stage-managed, and students may welcome the opportunity to socialise with fellow students online, where in a campus context they might meet in a bar.

SUMMARISING CONTACT WITH GROUPS AND INDIVIDUALS

I have discussed tutor-mediated support in the context of contacts with groups of students, as well as individuals, in both formal and informal contexts. In addition, there are often opportunities for students to support each other, either formally as part of a class or perhaps an assessable component, or more informally as part of a conversation or in an online conference. Table 2.3 provides a pictorial summary of contacts with groups and individuals, through formal and informal means.

Table 2.3 Summarising contact with groups and individuals

	Tutor with individual	Tutor with group	Student with student
Formal	Assignment feedback	Tutorials, practical work	Peer assessment
Informal	Individual needs	Keeping in touch	Peer support groups; mentoring

You might find it helpful to reflect on your own activity in supporting your students, and perhaps amend the table so that it describes your particular context. In which area is there the most activity? Are you aware of the significance and contribution of informal contacts? How could your students support each other more effectively? How might you improve on the balance of individual to group needs?

The deployment of online media for tutor-mediated support has meant that many of the traditional boundaries between formal and informal, or alternatively group and individual contact, have been eroded. For example:

- The use of an online conference, or perhaps email to a list, makes it relatively simple to share assignment feedback with a group, as well as, or instead of, giving it to individuals. We know that tutorials will in any case regularly cover material which is related either to the preparation of forthcoming assignments or to assignments which have recently been marked, so that they are effectively a part of formative feedback or feed-forward to the group. The SOLACE work indicated that there is probably considerable overlap in what tutor-mediated support is delivered through assignment feedback, and what is delivered through tutorials or through other routes. The use of an online conference for assignment related feedback or feed-forward could formalise that relationship.

- Individual queries received via email can readily be answered to the group, where they represent a common interest.
- Messages from the tutor to the group to keep in touch may invite further interaction between students using email where previously, using snail mail, they were essentially one-way communications.
- The use of online conferences may contribute significantly to the scope for students to help each other, although of course the difference may be far more important for distance students who otherwise have limited opportunities for meeting each other. There is scope not only for socialising and course-related discussion, but also for formal peer assessment.
- The synchronous alternatives to face-to-face tutorial work (whether using audio conferencing or online tools) tend to support smaller groups than are feasible face to face. And some of the functions traditionally associated with the tutorial may move into support to the individual, given on demand, rather than as programmed contact.

Such analysis leads one to reflect not only on the contribution of online media to a blended strategy, but also to the contribution of other, more traditional elements. Could we be using that tutorial time or lab time more productively within a blended strategy?

IN SUMMARY

I have introduced the SOLACE project as a way of illustrating an approach to reflection on the purpose of contact with students and use of the media. In doing this, I have probably posed far more questions than answers. I have made the following major points:

- Our project illustrated the use of a variety of tutor-mediated support strategies, which took place not only with the group but also with individuals in both formal and informal ways.
- A variety of media was deployed, including online asynchronous media, face to face, telephone, assignment feedback and paper mailing.
- In addition to tutor intervention, it was clear that students themselves initiated regular contact with staff and this had been facilitated by the advent of email.
- Campus and distance institutions have much in common in their use of a variety of strategies and media for supporting students. However, the

choice of strategy will vary with the environment and the availability or attractiveness of alternatives, and will also be determined by the curriculum and what is being taught.

- The introduction of online media is eroding traditional boundaries between support to the group and the individual, whether formally or informally. It is time to reassess what we do presently.

The next chapter continues this reflective theme, with a discussion of what tutors value in terms of the quality of particular intervention strategies, and how that relates to the use of asynchronous or synchronous media.

RESOURCE

Macdonald, J. and McAteer, E. (2003) New approaches to supporting students: strategies for blended learning in distance and campus-based environments. *Journal of Educational Media* **28** (2–3), pp. 129–146.

CHAPTER 3

TUTORS' PERCEPTIONS OF EFFECTIVE INTERVENTION

How do you choose which parts of the course might take place face to face, in a classroom or making use of alternative synchronous technologies? Which activities might benefit from discussion in an asynchronous environment like email or an online discussion forum? To what extent should you be using online media to replace a face-to-face tutorial or a practical session in a laboratory? Would you be achieving the same objectives if you did? What would be the effects on student learning, and which students might benefit the most? I believe it is helpful to turn the question around, by giving some careful thought to what you value in current practice and what you wish to achieve.

In Chapter 2 I described a tool which we developed for reflecting on current practice in supporting learners. The tutors who used this tool to record their activities were also asked to describe why they undertook interventions in that particular way. We wanted to establish what they saw as really effective high-quality intervention, and why.

This chapter outlines their views on quality in intervention, and then gives you an opportunity to test out your ideas on supporting your own students' learning. The approach here is to describe some objectives for supporting learning before considering the consequences for effective strategies and choice of media. It provides a framework for making decisions on blending synchronous and asynchronous support.

WHAT MAKES FOR GOOD QUALITY?

The following list summarises quality in intervention, based on comments made by the SOLACE participants on the reasons for their adoption of particular tuition and support strategies. I will discuss these aspects in more detail, and then go on to describe the ways in which the tutors were attempting to meet their objectives.

Quality in intervention

- affective – confidence building
- dialogic – tailoring to individual needs
- focusing – bringing study to the fore
- reflective – allowing time to think
- timely – arriving when relevant and useful
- reversionable – using support to individual as well as group
- accessible – available to maximum number of students.

Affective

An aspect of tutor-mediated support which the tutors valued greatly is the ability to engender confidence, and to build a working relationship with individual students. They described the conscious choice of media in order to meet these objectives. Synchronous contact, either face to face or by telephone, was important in this context (indeed, it is probably one of the most compelling reasons for a face-to-face tutorial or seminar) although clearly, continuous asynchronous contact through email or computer conferencing has also been helpful. Here are some comments from the tutors.

The feedback from the students on the day schools is that they find them a vital part of the course, in getting together to cover areas that have been causing problems in the course material, and also meeting and working as a group in sharing ideas, concerns, etc. I also find these meetings very important as they give me an opportunity for face-to-face communication rather than computer conferencing. (Business school tutor)

I like email: it is fast, but the feeling of group warmth and ongoing motivation comes from the human contact of face-to-face tutorials and telephone conference calls, and these provide the residual energy to drive forward the online activity I feel. (Humanities tutor)

When I was teaching an entirely online group for the first time ... my near constant presence on the tutorial conference meant they felt they knew me better than do the face-to-face students who see me only five times during the year, and hence they were less inhibited about phoning. (Technology tutor)

You will see that although they all refer to the importance of affective issues, they are not necessarily using the same medium or teaching strategy to get there.

Dialogic

It is often important for the tutor to tailor their intervention to particular and individual student needs, and to do this they need to be able to judge the extent of its effectiveness. In this context, many tutors underlined the importance of synchronous contact, whether by phone or face to face, as a way of establishing a dialogue, refining their support, and 'getting to the root of problems' which were not initially apparent. At the same time, it is clear that asynchronous contact through email or computer conferencing also has potential for interactivity and dialogue, albeit less powerful than synchronous contact, and is also presently in use in this context.

This is what some of the tutors had to say about dialogic issues:

> *I had one contact concerning a late assignment submission. When I quizzed her about what she had already done, I realised that she was on the wrong track so I discussed the idea of theory/perspectives and their inclusion into the essay (about 15/20 minutes).* (Social science tutor)

> *The emails were mostly going back and forth between one particular student and myself, starting with an administrative matter, concerning the downloading of an attachment on a previous email and going on to give feedback on the assignment. This student then asked for help with something for the next assignment.* (Science tutor)

Focusing

In the context of distance education, and indeed for campus-based institutions catering for part-time study, students will generally 'time share' study routines with jobs, family and other commitments. This means that for any individual student, the course is unlikely to be in focus at the same time as the rest of the tutorial group, unless there is some opportunity to meet. There is an argument here for creating a focus, when the course and study are brought to the fore at the same time for the whole group. In this context synchronous meetings, whether face to face, or using telephone or video conferencing, or real-time audiographics, can provide an effective complement to asynchronous conferencing.

> *When people are gathered together in one 'seminar' type activity at the same time ... then it provides a focus and imaginative engagement in which the whole is much greater than the parts, and part of that comes from not thinking about anything else during that time.* (Humanities tutor)

There are times when this can be particularly important, for example when there are decisions and tasks to be negotiated, perhaps at the outset of a collaborative activity.

Reflective

Almost the obverse of focusing is the view that it can be particularly valuable to be able to reflect on your contribution, either in terms of giving a considered response to students' comments or written work, or to give students the chance to reflect on their own responses. Related to this issue is the fact that some students will appreciate some flexibility in time and location to accommodate a variety of working practices and part-time study. In either case, the written medium (on paper, email or computer conference) has particular strengths because of its asynchronicity.

> It's nice to have time to compose a meaningful message rather than responding on the hoof – as in face to face or on the phone. (Social sciences tutor)

> The thing about online working is that activities can run in parallel. This gives students plenty to do when they log on and allows anyone who can't get on for a day or two to catch up. (Business school tutor)

Timely and relevant

Tutors commented on a surge of communications from students, particularly in relation to important events such as forthcoming assignments, and this illustrates how valuable an intervention can be if it is timed to occur when it is useful or relevant to the students' current needs.

Chapter 11 describes how assignments are highly significant in focusing attention on certain aspects of the course, and tutor interventions that relate to assignments currently in preparation are more likely to be well received than those which are not. In this context, all of the available media have been used to achieve this end, although electronic communication has the advantage of being rapid, and therefore highly responsive to the particular or local needs of a group.

> My students submit their examinable component in early October, so I sent them an email asking them about any final concerns/issues, problems and generally offering encouragement to complete. This provoked many phone calls and email responses. (Education tutor)

Reversionable

Very often the needs of identifiable individuals are reflected in those of other members of the group. The ability to reversion advice for sub-groups of students, while personalising it for a particular individual, can be a powerful strategy and is achievable in a variety of ways. Electronic media are particularly effective in this context, because of the use of cut and paste, but then so too is the traditional tutorial.

> *Using email I find it useful to copy the same message to a larger group. For example, after my last telephone tutorial with the Argyll group I could get feedback and also chased up an agreement about the next convenient date.* (Humanities tutor)

> *I don't think you can beat face-to-face contact because you can cover so many different aspects of student contact in one session. You can respond to students directly, making full use of different ways of learning, and encourage student interaction.* (Maths tutor)

Accessible

The question of providing support that is available to all students is of keen interest to tutors, particularly in a distance context. A variety of limitations are imposed by the situations of individual students, in terms of their geographical isolation; their access to online facilities, or perhaps to a landline telephone; and the obsolescence of hardware or software in the home or place of study. Students may also be restricted by their levels of competence and confidence in the necessary skills for studying using technologies.

For synchronous technologies, limitations are also imposed by the number of students which the tool can support. For example, the use of telephone conferencing and some real-time audiographics packages may only support small groups of six to eight students at one time. Such restrictions have led to the duplication of provision using a variety of media. Although the use of asynchronous online media (particularly computer conferencing) can provide a solution, the partial adoption of online media among the student population or their reluctance to log in regularly, exacerbates the dilemma.

> *I find telephone conferencing the most effective means of holding a tutorial for widely scattered students, as it is the most generally accessible medium.* (Technology tutor)

> *Over the next week I propose to phone the students (eight of them) who have neither read the conference posting nor attended the tutorial ... One thing I considered doing (but didn't) was trying to phone (before the tutorial) the students who have access to the conference but hadn't read the posting re the tutorial.* (Science tutor)

Arguably, it is this level of concern for the identifiable individual and an awareness of those who are not participating which keeps potentially failing students from dropping out. However, this has to be balanced against the resource implications.

INTERVENTION QUALITY AND MEDIA CHOICE

You may be wondering where all this reflection takes us. My first observation is that some of these qualities reflect previous work in the field; for example, the significance of affective support for maintaining student motivation, or the importance of dialogue for explaining difficult concepts. It is my feeling that the relative importance of others will depend on the context and the subject or discipline in question. At the same time, I believe it is a useful approach to concentrate the mind on objectives in intervention.

Second, it looks as if no single strategy using a particular medium will satisfy all these quality issues. We can expect to employ a range of strategies using a blend of media if we are to accommodate a diversity of student needs. And, clearly, an online tutorial differs in several important ways from a face-to-face tutorial: after all, it will probably be text-based, rather than spoken, and may be asynchronous, rather than synchronous.

Third, there is a variety of ways in which quality in intervention might be achieved, and the experiences of the tutors contributing to this study illustrate the fact that it would be foolish to formulate hard and fast rules. In general their choice of media reflected a division between synchronous and asynchronous intervention. So, drawing from their observations, face-to-face contact through tutorials or seminars may excel in terms of its affective contribution, interactivity, flexibility, and the fact that it provides a focus for the group. Where face-to-face contact is inappropriate, or impossible, other synchronous technologies that employ spoken or visual communication (such as telephone conferencing or desktop video conferencing) may offer similar advantages if they can be properly integrated as part of the teaching strategy. On the other hand, asynchronous media such as the online conference or email will often fulfil different roles to the synchronous tutorial in terms of their contribution to reflection, timeliness or flexibility, and they open up new options for tuition. There is nothing new in this kind of analysis. In fact, Laurillard (2002) introduced the concept of affordance of a medium, as a way of describing how different electronic tools may have the ability to contribute to the support of learning in different ways.

WHICH QUALITIES DO YOU VALUE?

You may wish to pause and consider how these qualities in intervention relate to your own situation. Table 3.1 summarises the issues discussed here, but it is not an exhaustive list and you might feel that other qualities are important to you. You could try completing the grid by adding any additional issues which you feel are relevant, and then assessing their relevance to yourself and your students. How do your present teaching strategies score on these qualities? What strategies and media might you use in the future?

Table 3.1   Your views on quality in intervention

Quality in intervention	Value to your students (1 = little value; 5 = extremely valuable)	How would you score your present strategies?	What new strategies might you choose?
Affective (confidence building)			
Dialogic (tailoring to student needs)			
Focusing (bringing study to the fore)			
Reflective and flexible (allowing time to think; providing for flexible working)			
Timely and relevant (arriving when relevant and useful)			
Reversionable (supporting both individual and group)			
Accessible (options and alternatives)			
Other?			

It is very likely that the importance which you attach to the items on this list will be dependent on a number of factors. You might like to make a note of the factors which you took into consideration when completing this table, before reading on. Here are my thoughts.

Contextual factors

These include:

- the availability and accessibility of alternatives;
- the students' previous educational experience and individual needs;
- whether you are concerned about student retention;
- the level of e-competence of students;
- their familiarity with self-directed study;
- the media available to you and your students;
- their access to Internet-ready equipment;
- their familiarity with written English;
- the model of tutorial support you intend to adopt;
- the amount of tutor time you intend to invest;
- the nature of the intervention: what it is designed to achieve;
- the tutors' experience of tools and new approaches;
- the scale of course presentation; and
- the course learning objectives and curriculum design.

Implications for media choice

You might wish to relate the ideas set out here on intervention quality to your own perceptions on the strengths of various media. Of course, there is no right answer here: your own views on their relative importance will be coloured by your situation, and that of your students.

Use a code for your responses:

Excellent	1
Acceptable	2
Poor	3
Useless	4
Don't know	5

In Table 3.2, I have put in my own ideas on the contribution of email, to start you off. But you are allowed to disagree with me!

Table 3.2   Choosing appropriate media

	Email	Computer conf.	Face to face	Texting; real-time chat	Tel. conf.	Audio graphics	Video conf.
Affective	3						
Dialogic	3						
Focusing	3						
Reflective	1						
Timely	1						
Reversionable	1						
Accessible	2						

IN SUMMARY

In this chapter I have described tutors' views on quality in intervention. Their perspectives underline the richness of tutor-mediated support, and the wide variety of factors which come into play. Clearly, a range of solutions is needed to address particular needs. By adopting blended strategies, integrating both synchronous and asynchronous contact, and using a range of media with both groups and individuals in an informed way, we will have the flexibility we need to support individuality and diversity in our students.

RESOURCE

Laurillard, D. (2002) *Rethinking University Teaching. A conversational framework for the effective use of learning technologies* (London, Routledge, second edition).

CHAPTER 4

BLENDED LEARNING AND PRAGMATISM

I have described what is happening in contacts between individual tutors and their students, and how that might impact on a choice of strategies and media. But what about the course designers: who is adopting blended learning, on which courses, with which students, and what influences their decisions? My aim in this chapter is to describe current practice in blended learning in a variety of institutions, and to illustrate the influence of the teaching and learning environment on decisions to adopt a blended strategy, using extracts from a range of case studies.

The work which underpins this chapter was undertaken with a grant from the Centre for Education and Educational Technology, Open University (UK), and my special thanks go to Sonja Cameron for her contribution in working with me in the analysis of the data.

A SURVEY OF CURRENT PRACTICE

At the end of 2004 we undertook a survey of current practice in blended learning, by posting a short questionnaire to a variety of academic mailing lists, and writing to individuals who were known to have presented papers on blended learning at a variety of conferences over the past year. Mailing lists have in recent years become established as a way of keeping in touch with academics in a wide variety of disciplines. They are favoured as a way of posting notices about forthcoming conferences and other events, job opportunities, and the occasional forum for debate, although such debate rarely extends beyond a couple of days. At any rate, they are accessed by large numbers of individuals across a wide variety of institutions, and they do not necessarily respect geographical boundaries. And since emails of interest are readily forwarded to colleagues, they potentially have a much wider readership than is formally joined to the list.

As with any input to an online conference where many of the readers are unknown to the writer, the initial stages of this survey were unnerving: there was a rash of acknowledgements, followed by silence, and then the arrival of fascinating and unexpected messages. While some individuals completed the questionnaire in some detail, others wrote briefly. Some correspondents wrote to contribute resources and useful websites and others engaged in protracted debate on the subject of blended learning. The whole experience was extremely valuable as a way of gaining an understanding of the major issues of concern, and we were able to reply to many respondents with further questions and points for clarification. The data which we have collected therefore are from an opportunistic sample of practitioners and staff developers who have first-hand experience of blended learning on their courses and who were willing to share their experiences. We received 48 case studies from 37 educational institutions in 17 countries. With the exception of responses from the Open University (UK), they represented campus-based institutions who were making use of distance education to a greater or lesser extent. The survey represents a self-selected group, who were not surprisingly blended learning enthusiasts. You will find a complete list of those who responded to the questionnaire, in Appendix 1.

From theology to tourism...

When courses with an online component were first introduced they were aimed primarily at postgraduate students, but this is no longer the case. In fact, two-thirds of our case studies described courses at undergraduate level, while a third described postgraduate courses and a further third described continuous professional development, or vocational training. In practice some courses were doing several jobs – providing both continuous professional development and a qualification at sub degree, degree or post degree level. Undergraduate students are now clearly expected to have, or to acquire, the kind of skills required for independent study previously attributed to postgraduates, and to derive benefits from a flexible learning environment.

As for subjects, we were not surprised to learn that a third of case studies were about courses on pedagogy or online pedagogy, as that is commonly where innovations in course design begin. In such cases the use of a blended learning environment is as much a part of the course content as it is the course environment. But our respondents also described courses in medicine and healthcare, management, computing, geology, in addition to theology, and tourism.

Strategies for lifelong learners

Three-quarters of the case studies we received described courses catering to mature students between the ages of 20 and 40, and that reflects a growth in the market for lifelong learners and no doubt a recognition that they have particular needs. That is not very surprising, after all, lifelong learners are more likely than younger school-leavers to appreciate the flexibility offered by the asynchronous elements in a blended strategy.

COMMON COMPONENTS OF BLENDED LEARNING

The two commonest components of blended learning referred to by our respondents were asynchronous conferencing and face-to-face contact, and that reflects current assumptions on what blended learning is about. The somewhat motley collection of responses in the chart are a reflection of the fact that our questions were open-ended and exploratory. By and large, they reflect the use of particular technologies rather than what people did with them. Some of the responses we received referred to content delivery, some referred to tutor-mediated or automated support and some referred to a combination of the two.

For example, asynchronous conferencing, referred to by most respondents, is essentially a form of tutor-mediated or peer support. Support was also delivered using email, telephone and various synchronous online tools including realtime chat and whiteboards. We believe the number of cases referring to email is probably an under-representation, since we suspect many people do not associate informal un-programmed contact with individual students as part of teaching strategy, and therefore omitted to mention it.

Face-to-face contact in tutorials, seminars or labs is again a form of tutor mediated support, although as you will see from the extracts, in some case studies it meant lectures, which are arguably a combination of content delivery and support. A similar case might be made for videoconferencing – that might be used for a lecture, or for a more facilitative type of approach.

In addition to tutor mediated support, there were references to automated forms of support, delivered through, for example, online quizzes and formative assessment packages.

Finally, respondents referred to content delivery through print materials or a variety of web-based resources, including PowerPoint slides or digital multimedia.

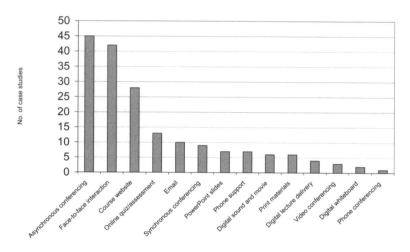

Figure 4.1   Components of blended learning

THE TEACHING AND LEARNING ENVIRONMENT

Inevitably, the observations I am going to make here have much in common with many other studies which have examined the adoption of online media in post secondary education. The difference to my mind is in the growing recognition of the significance of the *context* in which these changes take place, and often a concern not to lose what was good in traditional approaches to supporting students.

We were able to identify three teaching and learning contexts in which blended learning was introduced. You will see that these categories overlap somewhat, and clearly they all have certain aspects in common. I have chosen to focus on the status of the course or programme in terms of whether it was intended for campus-based, distance, or both campus and distance students, rather than the status of the institution as a whole. In our survey we estimated that 23 case studies represent courses for campus-based students, while 18 were courses for distance students and seven were courses for both. The following account describes these three contexts and the pragmatic concerns of course designers in adopting blended learning. I hope it will give you an opportunity to compare your own situation with theirs.

Courses for campus-based students

Formal support to the group is traditionally delivered through face-to-face synchronous contact for both content delivery, discussion or the practising of skills, whether through lectures, seminars, tutorials or lab sessions. In terms of informal opportunities for contact both with the group and with individuals, students may also be able to rely on face-to-face meetings either with staff or fellow students.

In order to accommodate variations in study patterns imposed by students' work-based or other commitments, or the pressure from growing student numbers or other constraints, course designers have adopted online media as part of a blended strategy. Such strategies are commonly associated with the redeployment of contact time, with the substitution of some of the face-to-face time, whether in lectures or tutorials, with self-study printed or web-based resources, in addition to introducing opportunities for discussion through asynchronous computer conferencing. There are two elements to this change: the introduction of online media; and the occasional or partial separation, and sometimes partial asynchronicity, in content delivery and tutor-mediated support.

At the same time, there is an awareness that face-to-face contact remains an important part of teaching strategy: in a campus-based environment this is relatively straightforward to accommodate at certain points in the course. Not only does it contribute to the formal support delivered to the group, it also has advantages in terms of informal opportunities for support. On the other hand, if face-to-face contact is readily available to students, then asynchronous discussion can be less attractive. Here are four extracts from the case studies we received. You will see that after each extract in this chapter and elsewhere in the book I include a number, which refers to the specific case study, and the name of the institution (see Appendix 1 for full details of each case study).

Third Year Manufacturing Operations Management. The class runs with half the formal contact time than originally. This formal contact time is for structuring and addressing key concepts. The students use a commercial CD pack for their main studies, as well as complementary online interactive web materials to address the areas that the CDs don't address. Overall contact time remains the same as there are workshop/lab-based sessions to support the students in individual or group settings as they carry out their learning in an independent and flexible manner. The students carry out an international team project with half the group from Strathclyde and half from Iowa State in the USA. The assignment draws heavily on the experience and technology of the DIDET project (used for the team design project). Students use LLE [Laulima Learning Environment] to communicate, share data, manage the project and use the (Iowa State) Engineering Learning Portal (ELP) to retrieve the assignment and submit their solution. Students work collaboratively and asynchronously with face-to-face and email support from the US and UK tutors (4, Univ. Strathclyde, UK)

Since 1999–2000, the traditional face-to-face approach of the course 'instructional science' was redesigned in response to recent concerns with regard to the traditional face-to-face approach of education at Ghent University. Due to the growing number of students, it was questioned how qualitative education could be guaranteed in an active way and educational support could be provided to a large number of first year students. The introduction of a blended learning environment, combining face-to-face sessions and asynchronous discussion groups, was seen as a way out. Basic aims of the redesign were: fostering 'active learning', giving students continuous support, fostering the 'application' of declarative and procedural knowledge, and developing self-evaluation skills of students. The redesign involved three subsequent phases. First, the approach focused on the blending of asynchronous discussion groups and face-to-face sessions. Since collaboration scripts are considered as powerful means to improve processes and outcomes of collaborative learning, in a next phase roles were introduced as a scripting tool to optimise the learning environment. The third phase focused on introducing cross-age tutors in asynchronous discussion groups to support the freshmen's discourse ... Students work together by applying the theoretical concepts of the course to solve problems presented in the online environment. In line with the constructivist principles, the problems are based on real-life authentic situations. (12, Ghent Univ., Belgium)

For the blended courses the students attended the university for the first four weeks of a 12-week course; it was made clear to them from the beginning that the website was theirs, that we would be working in a paperless classroom and that I would be teaching from the website, which had all the documentation such as course handbooks that we would normally print and copy for them, plus lecture notes etc. The students were all given the opportunity to log onto the site and use the interactive learning materials under my guidance. I explained that for four weeks of the course they would not be expected to attend the university but could work from home, if they had a computer (all did), or from the university's computer labs. For the weeks at home there would be computer-based interactive activities plus a discussion forum. Students were initially nervous about the whole idea but came to enjoy the experience, and the course was very well evaluated, with students saying they felt more confident about the technology and would like to use this form of learning again and quite possibly take the wholly computer-based versions of the course. (22, Univ. of Greenwich, UK)

The blended strategy became the only option due to the complexity of the module taught. Initially it was the pure distance between my resources. The module is run in two campuses located in Hendon and Trent Park, both in North London with a good 30-45 minutes driving between depending on traffic. Lectures, labs and seminars would take place for different groups of students based on the different campuses. Furthermore, next semester a remote Hong Kong campus will be teaching this particular module based on my guidelines through the virtual learning environment (VLE). There are two lectures, 8 seminars and 8 lab sessions running each week. Each student has to attend one lecture and a seminar or lab depending on the week of study. There are two academics acting as seminar tutors who I meet every week to decide on schedule and content. Obviously the module's logistics are a nightmare. The amount of queries, clarifications and questions is enormous. The need to be consistent in all sessions, considering that overall three academics are involved, is also a drawback. Deadlines and submissions can be a pain and there was the question of ensuring that weekly tasks and the overall group project could be submitted, checked and provided with feedback on equal terms. (9, Middlesex Univ., UK)

Courses exclusively for distance students

For those courses catering exclusively for distance students, the default is that the students are not on campus. Indeed, there may not even be a campus. Students are often widely distributed, either geographically or temporally, and may study from home, or in spare periods during their working day. Arguably, these students may need greater flexibility in their study routines than those who are essentially campus-based. In fact flexibility is one of the major reasons why people sign up to study distance courses in the first place. Such students rely traditionally on an asynchronous study environment in which content is delivered through self-study materials, and tutor-mediated support takes place through correspondence tuition supplemented with occasional face-to-face tutorials or telephone conversations. This means that formal support is delivered largely to the individual, with some group support available to some students and few opportunities for informal contact. Garrison and Anderson (2003) describe this context:

> *... it is also true that the context within which education is practised affects design and practice. The distance education context is complicated by many factors, including: the mediation effects of the delivery and communication media; the lack of physical proximity and body language used for feedback in classrooms; the lack of instructor perception and control over the actual learning environment; the difficulty of authentication and privacy in distributed contexts; and the reduction of informal, after-class interaction in some forms of distance delivery.* (Garrison and Anderson, 2003, p. 93)

The adoption of online media, including the availability of additional course resources, email and computer conferencing, have made it possible not only to maintain contact and community between synchronous tutorials, but also to provide opportunities for collaborative work and peer support which would not otherwise be feasible. At the same time, there is a recognition that it is best supplemented by face-to-face contact, or synchronous alternatives such as the telephone or real-time chat, although that is not always feasible.

Together with four other teachers I received funding from the Norwegian authorities to develop a new course for physical therapists, based on learning on demand. The course is called Medical Exercise Therapy. It is a part-time further education programme of 15 ECT (European credits) given over five months. Our target group was physiotherapists working at departments of rehabilitation or private training institutes with training equipment. To meet their needs, we set up a programme with assignments that required collaboration and sharing of experience from their clinical practice. The teaching strategy was to bring practitioners from all over Scandinavia together in a virtual learning community, to discuss how they examine patients, plan treatment and evaluate outcomes. They were given some resources (articles) when they participated at a physical meeting in Bergen ... The first time we tried out this model of teaching (spring 2003), we intended to run [online] synchronous meetings each week with tutorial support. We soon experienced that this was not possible to organise, since the students could not be logged on at regular intervals. We abandoned this strategy and found it sufficient to give our feedback at convenient occasions, asynchronously. (1, Bergen Univ. College, Norway)

Two of the most significant problems in the training of emigrant teachers is their extended geographic dispersal and the lack of a system of lifelong learning, which would provide support to teachers in the countries in which they live. The whole project PAIDEIA OMOGENWN (http://ediamme.edc.uoc.gr/diaspora/) aims to continue, develop and promote Greek language and culture, to primary and secondary students of Greek origin, who live and study abroad, as well as non-Greek speaking students who want to learn the Greek language and become participants in the Greek culture. Based on the suggested methodology, Greek teachers abroad were separated into target groups, depending on their ability to make use of computers and the Internet ... The third group comprises teachers who both possess basic ICT skills and have access to the Internet. Our effort concerns the implementation of a complete web-based learning environment, focusing on the third group and particularly on countries such as the USA, Canada and Australia. The proposed instructional model suggests the functional combination ... of educational technologies of synchronous (videoconferences) and asynchronous learning (web-based learning platform) ... in order to provide an interactive learning environment for Greek teachers in the countries they live in. (2, Univ. Crete, Greece)

The three online courses featured from the CREATE portfolio ... are currently delivered through the Suffolk Institute of Technology ... These courses involve no physical contact between tutors and students and the 'blend' is between pure e-learning delivery and verbal contact and support. Learning is supported by a Virtual Learning Environment and learners receive academic and pastoral support from subject tutors and personal tutors respectively via telephone. Technical assistance is also available via the same medium. Students on these courses are geographically dispersed throughout the UK. (19–21, Suffolk College, UK)

Courses for campus-based as well as distance students

The third and final context is where courses cater for both campus-based and distance students at the same time. This dual-mode provision has been common in Australian universities for some years, but we also received responses from courses in European universities and colleges which follow this model. Such courses create particular issues for staff workload associated with a need to provide for consistency and equity of access across campus and distance delivery. Formal support may be delivered to the group in the case of the campus-based students, and to individuals in the case of distance students. Informal opportunities for contact are probably common for one part of the cohort, and problematic for the others.

The introduction of online media within a blended strategy allows for the use of common teaching materials for both campus and distance students, and a common web-based interface can be deployed to link distance students with those who were able to attend face-to-face classes, or to provide opportunities for collaborative study which had previously not been possible. At the same time, some have found that certain campus-based students prefer the flexibility of distance learning, if given the choice.

While face-to-face or synchronous alternatives are still recognised as a significant part of the strategy, students are offered a choice, and it is recognised that it will rarely be possible to accommodate all distance and campus-based students at one time. In this case, asynchronous provision, both in terms of content and tutor-mediated support, enhanced by synchronous contact is adopted in order to provide choice and equal access for students with a variety of needs.

Over the last decade, and in line with Griffith University policy, academics within the AVE [Adult and Vocational Education] area: (1) moved towards offering a reduced suite of core courses from which all of the programmes draw, (2) moved to offer all programmes in a 'flexible' mode making the area unique within Griffith. The move to flexible delivery has taken place during a time when significant changes in demographics and patterns of study have occurred within our student cohort. A decade ago our student cohort comprised a significant full-time, on-campus group as a result of an employer-supported teacher education programme. They were taught face-to-face, on-campus in a lock-step mode. The demise of that employer support, together with changes in the Vocational Education and Training (VET) environment, has seen our cohort becoming increasingly diverse, with many students having to juggle work and family commitments alongside study. The AVE concept of 'flexible' refers to both delivery and mode. Students may attend on-campus tutorials, tele-tutorials or study at a distance, that is in face-to-face, print and online modes. (40, Griffith Univ., Australia)

A blended learning approach was adopted following some serious discussions as how to best support and facilitate student learning for what is likely to be a geographically diverse cohort. We were also very aware, from discussions with our industry partners and from our own market research, that we needed to accommodate full- and part-time students as well as those wishing to undertake individual modules for CPD. This potential mix of students and geographical locations ruled out the use of tried and tested networked learning technologies such as video conferencing. All our modules will have between 12 and 15 lectures digitally recorded and merged with a lecture PowerPoint to be delivered via CD-ROM to each of the students prior to the start of the module in question. These programmes are delivered for use with an Internet browser which makes it very accessible as there is no expensive software required. These CD-ROM lectures will be complemented by paper packs and/or electronic materials developed for use within a Virtual Learning Environment. Students will also be expected to contribute to online discussion and chatrooms on a regular basis. We are currently exploring the use of software solutions for supporting live online discussions using webcams, etc. (5, Univ. Highlands & Islands Millennium Institute, UK)

We have a small-scale approach to distant courses. The distant students of the university are spread in a big (rural) area. They wish both f2f (face-to-face) and real-time (synchronous) meetings via some chosen technical tool, such as videoconference in studio or computer-based videoconference – more than real-time chat functions. Synchronous meetings for teaching, discussions, presentations, seminars, etc. are regular in the distant courses. There is a development of offering net-based courses for both campus students and distant students in the same courses. Using flexible, blended, net-based (or DE: distance education) comes naturally, as long as we are flexible about the technology, which is only the tool for teaching and learning at a distance. (44, Univ. Lulea, Sweden)

- *The course is about the use of technology in education. Students learn by first-hand involvement.*
- *Flexibility for students – many work or live at a distance.*
- *Catering for both internal and external environments including students overseas.*
- *Provides choices for them in the way they want to be supported – can choose to have support through weekly lab sessions OR email/phone contact, encouraging them to take responsibility for their own strategies.*
- *Students are at vastly different levels in terms of their own skills. Putting all students together in the same learning environment is considered inappropriate.*
- *Students are responsible for setting their own goals and choose their own pathway through the content, and are encouraged to draw on all sorts of learning supports and contexts. This flexibility is all part of the approach.* (32, Southern Cross Univ., Australia)

Summarising the teaching and learning environment

I have tried to summarise here my comments on the three teaching and learning environments, and the pragmatic concerns which our respondents described as underlying the adoption of their blended strategies.

Table 4.1   **Pragmatic concerns on the adoption of blended learning**

Students	Default	Influences on adoption of asynchronous strategies	Influences on retention of synchronous strategies
Campus-based	Synchronous study (face-to-face) for content delivery and support to group. Informal networks happen naturally	Achieves more flexibility. But may be less attractive to students than f-to-f alternatives	F-to-f contact relatively easy to organise for the group
Distance	Asynchronous support to individuals, some opportunities for synchronous support to group. Informal networks difficult	More continuous contact, and opportunities for collaborative working. A new option, rather than replacement. Informal networks possible	Any synchronous contact with whole group difficult; but can offer choice, or support to individuals
Campus plus distance	Synchronous to group for on campus and mostly asynchronous support for distance. Informal networks difficult for distance students	Equal access for all. More opportunities for collaborative working online, and for establishing informal networks	Problematic for whole group; but can offer choice, or support to individuals

I wonder if you recognise your own teaching and learning environment here? To what extent do these pragmatic reasons influence your blended strategy?

The three teaching and learning environments I have described here all start from different positions, and the experience of being a student in these three contexts will be different, although you might see them as part of a continuum. Although they all refer to blended learning, in practice it is much more difficult to provide opportunities for synchronous tutor-mediated support for distance students than it is for campus-based students. Although the technology might be the same in both contexts, it might be more difficult to entice campus-based students to contribute to asynchronous computer conferences than distance students when they have other opportunities to discuss the course in face-to-face seminars.

There are parallels to draw with other work we have undertaken recently. In Chapter 2, I described a comparative study of tutor support in distance and campus-based environments. While both institutions made use of blended learning, the acceptability and feasibility of particular strategies depended partly on differences in the overall teaching and learning environment and the availability of alternatives.

There is obviously much variation both in the ways and extent to which respondents to the blended learning survey adopted asynchronous, or face-to-face or online synchronous strategies. In fact, some course designers used online resources or conferencing in a supporting role to traditional lectures and seminars. This reflects previous studies, for example one of VLE use in UK campus-based universities, where the online component was commonly used as a 'gateway to materials', including course outlines, assignment guidelines, links to useful resources, or lecture handouts (Morón-García, 2004). On the other hand, some respondents in the present survey had transformed their pedagogic approach. Indeed, several referred to the use of problem-based learning as part and parcel of their blended strategy.

Harasim (2000) refers to the use of online media in *adjunct mode*, to enhance traditional face-to-face or distance education; or alternatively in *mixed mode*, in which a significant portion of traditional classroom work takes place online; or finally *totally online*, which is self-explanatory. I think blended learning commonly belongs in the first two of those categories, although you could argue that if 'totally online' means the use of both asynchronous and synchronous media, then it belongs there too.

In spite of these differences in approach, there are common characteristics in blended strategies which apply, to a greater or lesser extent, across all three teaching and learning contexts, and I will go on to describe these characteristics, and the implications for student learning in the next chapter.

IN SUMMARY

I have made the following points in this chapter:

- In courses for campus-based students, the need to provide more flexibility to accommodate student diversity and a variety of study routines imposed by students' work-based and other commitments has led to a demand for asynchronicity in course design. This has been fuelled by the widespread availability and adoption of asynchronous online media, and accompanied by the occasional separation of content delivery from tutor-mediated support. At the same time, there is recognition that face-to-face contact remains a significant part of teaching strategy, and it is relatively easy to organise for all.
- In courses for distance students, where flexibility and consequently asynchronicity and choice have always been important, the adoption of online media, in particular email and conferencing, has meant that students can remain in touch on a more continuous basis than ever before. They can also work collaboratively, where previously they were unable to do so. At the same time it is recognised that face-to-face or online synchronous contact is important, although that is often difficult to achieve for whole student groups.
- For dual mode courses, the adoption of online asynchronous media allows for consistency of provision across both contexts, and means that students can remain in touch regardless of their location. While synchronous contact is regarded as important, it is more feasible to arrange for face-to-face contact for campus-based students than it is for distance students.

RESOURCES

Garrison, D.R. and Anderson, T. (2003) *E-learning in the Twenty-first Century. A framework for research and practice* (London, Routledge Falmer).

Harasim, L. (2000) Shift happens: Online education as a new paradigm in learning. *The Internet and Higher Education* **3** (1–2), pp. 41–61.

Morón-García, S. (2004) *Understanding lecturers' use of virtual learning environments to support face-to-face teaching in UK higher education* (unpublished doctoral thesis, Open University, UK).

CHAPTER 5

BLENDED LEARNING AND PEDAGOGY

Many people have observed how beneficial variety can be in a course of study. It can often enliven the whole experience of learning, particularly for students who are studying on their own. But do course designers deploy online asynchronous and face-to-face reviews because they support learning in different ways? The aim of this chapter is to discuss present practice in using online asynchronous and face-to-face or online synchronous environments, as it is described in the case studies of blended learning.

THE CONTRIBUTION OF ASYNCHRONOUS SUPPORT

There is a rich and extensive literature on the potential contribution of asynchronous online support to student learning. It is claimed that it presents opportunities to develop independent self-directed learners, providing a good foundation for lifelong learning, and in some cases offering greater choice to students and a wider range of teaching approaches. It offers a greater scope for reflection than is possible in face-to-face environments; provides access to wider, more readily updated resources; and some writers claim that it can enhance learner engagement and a sense of community. According to Collis:

> *... students not only have a wider choice of resources and modalities of study materials from which to choose ... but also come to share in the responsibility of identifying appropriate additional resources for the course and even contributing to the learning resources in a course.* (Collis, 1998, p 377)

Of course, the extent to which any of this is achievable in practice is another matter. The environment may offer potential, but a wide variety of factors will influence the success of the strategy. The bottom line is that asynchronous environments give you more time to think, and when online they commonly use a written medium, so an asynchronous discussion will offer a qualitatively different experience to a verbal discussion in a classroom.

The respondents to the present survey were clearly aware of the potential of asynchronous media, and they were certainly alive to the opportunities presented for new teaching and learning approaches. The following extracts illustrate a diversity of ways in which asynchronous online environments were in use as part of their blended strategies.

> *For the first two years of this module, it had been delivered entirely online ... The actual learning situation entailed interpersonal complexities and subjective depths of meaning that challenged my assumptions about how problem-based learning would happen online .... In the light of these problems, it was decided to adopt a blended approach to delivery in that weekly face-to-face problem-based learning tutorials would be supported by online learning events e.g. exploration of online resources, collaborative research, online reflective journaling, self and peer assessment. The module web site was the hub that held the participants together outside of the once weekly f2f PBL tutorial. The activities were designed to scaffold the participant's learning: they began with a few individual activities, moved to pair work, then to working collaboratively in groups of four. (18, Dublin Inst. of Technology, Ireland; Donnelly, 2004))*

> *Through giving on-campus students the opportunity to communicate via the asynchronous electronic discussion forum they could extend their length of time in discussion of class-room topics. This resulted in the level and amount of dialog being much higher than otherwise. The couple of online students benefited from being able to participate with the discussions involving the on-campus students. (27, Australian Lutheran College, Australia)*

> *The module initially ran face to face, then was written into paper-based distance learning with optional face-to-face seminars because of demand for the module from distance students. Blackboard was initially used for support, but is now an integral part of the module to allow collaborative and situated learning which is necessary to develop expertise in specialist clinical practice.*
>
> *Blackboard use is designed to facilitate a community of practice. Tasks are constructivist and authentic, being based on scenarios from clinical practice where students can learn from each others' experience and debate solutions. Activities are primarily computer conferencing but also PowerPoint student seminar presentations, bad practice photographs, provision of additional, up-to-date resources, formative quizzes and an online portfolio developed by students from work-based activities. (30, Univ. Dundee, UK)*

> *The system is tightly designed to mirror and support the discovery process in PBL without contradicting the overall philosophy. It is also essentially blends in the students' learning of evidence-based medicine. All future doctors and dentists have to be not only familiar with IT, but also to be sophisticated users, so it seemed essential to support their skills from day 1 of the program. We also provide obvious things like timetables, outlines of teaching sessions and an open access, on-line self-assessment system which is well used, and*

conduct evaluations on-line ... Throughout the program, information technology is used to deliver the teaching and learning and to provide a means by which students can access medical literature and databases. These resources include text descriptions and outlines of the problems and associated lectures and laboratory sessions, moving and still medical images (radiology, pathology, histology, etc.), clinical data relevant to the problem of the week, Internet sites related to the problem, and on-line self-assessment questions and answers. (41, Univ Sydney, Australia; http://www.gmp.usyd.edu.au/vguide/index.)

In this respect, the online discussions do not replace the face-to-face discussions, but both collaborative approaches run parallel. The main goal for introducing the online discussion groups was to expand students' opportunities to get in touch with each other in order to discuss and reflect on medical cases. Face-to-face discussions focus on the diagnostic process and start from the patients' presenting problem. Asynchronous e-discussions focus on treatment options and informing the patient/parents and start from a complete case description with a given diagnosis. Furthermore, asynchronous text-based discussions present several advantages as compared to face-to-face discussions when discussing treatment options: students get more equal opportunities to contribute and students have more time to reflect, to think, and search for extra information before contributing to the discussion. (13, Univ. Ghent, Belgium)

THE CONTRIBUTION OF FACE-TO-FACE SUPPORT

There is very little in the literature to draw on, when trying to establish exactly what face-to-face support might contribute to a blended strategy. Of course, face-to-face support is a teaching strategy which has always been there, and perhaps the benefits are considered too obvious to be recognised. As the traditional approach in college or university education, it is probably an area where staff have the most experience, whether in tutorials, seminars, labs, or lectures. But with the enthusiasm engendered by the potential of online media, I believe it is timely to reflect on the wide variety of ways in which face-to-face contact can support learning, so that we can optimise its use. We should be wary of assuming that a face-to-face session within a blended strategy will necessarily fulfil the same functions as it did previously. After all, what differences will there be for students who have met each other online, or perhaps who have used resources on the web to further their knowledge and understanding beyond course materials?

Turning now to the respondents to our survey, while most recognised that the face-to-face element was important, few articulated clearly what its contribution for student learning might be. They described a wide variety of contexts in which face-to-face contact was presently deployed, and it has been possible to make some inferences from their comments.

Face-to-face sessions were valuable for the focusing of content, or the targeting of advice, particularly where the subject matter was particularly complex or difficult to understand, and this reflects comments by the OU tutors in Chapter 3, who appreciated a dialogic approach to tutor-mediated support, which allowed them to assess the extent to which the students understood course concepts.

Others referred to the pacing of studies, where face-to-face contact provided an introduction or conclusion to the course, and an occasion for final coursework presentations; or otherwise a goal towards which the students might concentrate their efforts.

Finally, some commented on its contribution to community building, or for brainstorming, or decision making, or for group formation, all of which is of particular relevance where students are expected to engage in collaborative projects. I have chosen a few extracts to illustrate these points, and have tried to indicate what roles I believe face-to-face contact serves in each example. You will see that in many cases it seems to have a variety of roles.

Targeting advice or focusing content; brainstorming; pacing of studies

The didactic concept of the Leipziger Online-Seminar is to link the theoretical basis of media literacy with the practical realisation of projects to gain media literacy. The whole seminar constitutes of two online phases and two meetings in real life. The two meetings in real life take place in the middle and at the end of the seminar. They are conducted as intensive two-day-workshops and fulfil two functions ... After the students gained the theoretical basis during the first online phase, the meeting in real life is used to repeat, deepen and control their knowledge. Beside that the first meeting in real life serves as a bridge to the second online phase, which aims at practical concepts. The students have to form new working groups related to different tasks. The first meeting in real life is the foundation for the following working in the course. Moreover, it serves as an impetus to start creative processes ... The second meeting marks the end of the seminar. The students present their developed concepts to the whole group ... Beside that, the second meeting serves as evaluation of the whole seminar, for which the communication situation as a face-to-face contact is good for. (15, Univ. Leipzig, Germany)

Enhancing community; targeting advice

Students constantly requested face-to-face sessions to provide additional training and support ... in terms of benefits, e-moderators noted that blended e-learning allowed the students to meet, develop relationships and a community spirit. (26, Univ. Glamorgan, UK; Miller, C. et al, 2004)

Pacing of studies

The 'real blended' policy was more easy applicable in this project where two different universities in two different countries are working together. Further two German consultants are involved and several companies will take part in the project. The ' blended ' structure of this project is: on-line (gathering personal information , information about the project and theory/resources/planning and organising the first F2F meeting in the Netherlands). F2F – kick off in the Netherlands – three days in October (students/lecturers from both institutes/ external experts Germany and one Dutch company). On-line (discussions, desk research individual end per group, contacting the companies, meetings, running the project). F2F – December (meetings: all different group will have meetings)

On-line (applied research and visiting the participating companies/writing the research report and results – shared documents/planning and organising the last F2F meeting in Germany). F2F – corporate events – presentation of the findings. (47, INHOLLAND Univ., Holland)

Targeting advice or focusing content

We generally have an introductory tutorial, which is face to face. In six-month course, there will be four tutorials, in 12-month courses there are eight, plus a day-school, where the curriculum demands it, e.g. for finance, there is a finance day-school as we recognise that is where students may experience difficulties ... or if there is a need for skills development best met by a sustained period of contact, or best met through a wider networking opportunity, for example, inter-personal skills, interviewing, that sort of thing. (34, Open Univ., UK)

Targeting advice or focusing content

First year programming modules are often found difficult by students, a blended approach gives support through online resources as well as the more familiar face-to-face methods. (33, Bolton Inst., UK)

Pacing of studies; targeting advice or focusing content

As the course is about e-learning, it seems both appropriate and necessary that participants experience this for themselves. Various methods of delivery have been explored during previous courses, including workshops and distance elearning. To date ... the face-to-face elements have been encouraged but not made compulsory. The course begins with an optional face-to-face workshop and then continues online ... Tutor support is provided by a combination of email, telephone and face-to-face meetings. Tutorials are usually based around project support ... At the end of the course participants share their projects in a face-to-face session ... During the last cohort the face-to-face tutorials were emphasised more, as participants often need such targeted advice for their project to progress ... At the end of the course participants share their projects in a face-to-face session. (11, Univ. Manchester, UK)

Enhancing community; pacing of studies

... it was clear that the essence of learning in this context is not about content available on-line or anywhere else, but is about the sense of 'community' and contact that the students get in some shape or form. Hence we have two introductory days at the start of the course, and then optional study days every six months ... where the teacher contact is structured around reflective/evidence-based practice issues. These are themed during the course, and students are encouraged to discuss the developments of their projects/presentation in class on the discussion board, i.e. sharing info and pooling resources. This option point was to acknowledge that if students cannot travel, they are not excluded from the learning materials, but simply don't get F2F support – only electronic mediated support ... We also have clinical training organised in the nurses own renal unit that is facilitated in a work-based learning structure ... [in the VLE] we use discussions (targeted from points in the materials), chatrooms (for informal student chat as well as online tutorials), video clips (to demo clinical skills), quizzes (to help self-directed learning, and help the staff understand the progress of the students) (24, City Univ., UK)

These extracts describe a variety of reasons for deploying face-to-face support at significant points. Some case studies described an initial induction session; others had a face-to-face session at the start and end of the course; and some had sessions at regular intervals throughout the course. The reasons for this variation were related to the pragmatic issues I discussed in the last chapter, but there were also factors associated with course structure, student needs and the nature of the learning objectives.

Whatever the frequency of use of face-to-face sessions, the evidence on student retention, and student attitudes to online courses certainly supports the view that face-to-face, or alternatively online synchronous support has an important contribution to make on some courses with some students. We know that some students who study exclusively online (meaning asynchronously) suffer feelings of isolation and falling motivation. Indeed, the importance of establishing relationships, through both formal and informal interactions, in contributing to social and academic integration, is well documented as critical for student retention. Simpson (2000) refers to the need for affective, as well as cognitive or organisational skills in supporting learners. In the end, the significance of synchronicity in this context may depend on the degree to which students are used to working independently, and the amount of support which they expect or perhaps need in order to keep on course and in tune. That, in turn, will depend on issues such as the course level and the previous educational experience of the students.

PEDAGOGY MEETS PRAGMATISM

With such a wide range of benefits ascribed to student learning in face-to-face environments, one wonders how distance students can possibly be supported effectively. The fact is that the ever-present need to offer learners maximum flexibility in their studies often makes any kind of synchronous meeting for the whole group difficult to organise. Luckily, some of the benefits ascribed to face-to-face learning may be achievable in other ways, and distance institutions have a range of responses to the dilemma. For example, while face-to-face meetings are often valued for the pacing of studies, an alternative way of achieving this in distance contexts is regular coursework which focuses on key course concepts and sets students deadlines and goals, and this strategy is a common feature in many distance institutions.

In addition, on some courses synchronous support is provided to individuals, often using the telephone either on demand or proactively as an alternative provision to the group, thus overcoming the difficulty of getting everyone together at one time.

Finally, a range of online tools can be deployed as a partial substitute for face-to-face meetings, and they are currently in use on some courses. Such tools may reduce some of the geographical hurdles to synchronous meetings, but unfortunately often replace these hurdles with technological difficulties. I discuss the ways in which synchronous support can be delivered using these tools in Chapter 8.

A case study from the University of the West Indies explains that they are planning to dispense with synchronous meeting via audio-conferencing completely. At the Open University (UK), while provision continues to be made for synchronous contact, students are often given a choice of alternatives.

UWI already employs a mixed delivery mode for its distance offerings, with pre-packaged print materials at the core, supported by face-to-face tutorials and audio conferencing. However, 'blended learning' offers the opportunity to assess the effectiveness of the existing 'mix' ... to move distance delivery away from synchronous modes, and in particular the audio conference component. With steadily increasing enrolment and number of courses, synchronous delivery is impractical ... Ultimately, UWIDEC would like to have a teaching-

learning system that is truly time and place independent, while still having high levels of interaction. (28, Univ. West Indies, Trinidad & Tobago)

For most synchronous technologies, including webcasts and IM, there were problems with firewalls. You need flexibility in the course approach if not all students can use these technologies ... Audience and subject matter meant that they were quite willing to tolerate unstable technologies – it was part of the learning. The Learning Object approach helped, as it contained the risk – if one bit didn't work, it didn't affect the whole course. They didn't have to do everything, e.g. some found IM intrusive – they didn't have to do it. It provided an element of choice. (46, Open Univ., UK)

IN SUMMARY

A discussion on good practice in blended learning is a bit like playing a game of three-dimensional noughts and crosses, because of the ways in which different parts of the strategy relate to each other. I have been able to show how the participants in this study had adopted asynchronous media, and the occasional, or partial separation of content and tutor-mediated support; and were aware of the importance of retaining face-to-face or online synchronous support at certain parts of the course.

However, I think we still have much to learn about the ways in which asynchronous and synchronous tutor-mediated support can be designed to complement each other. In particular, I believe we need to learn more about the contribution of face-to-face or technology-mediated synchronous contact as part of a blended strategy. We have tended to assume that we know the answer to this, and in an increasingly resource-conscious environment it becomes important to be more overt, not only about its benefits but also how its role might change for students who are networked at other times. And, if we really believe that synchronous contact is of central importance for students on some courses, then it cannot be an optional part of a blended strategy. The range of approaches to synchronous support I have described here really epitomises the thinking behind blended learning. If there is currently a recipe for a blended strategy, it is a broth of pedagogy, heavily peppered with pragmatism.

Having discussed blended learning with respect to asynchronous and synchronous tutor-mediated support for blended learning, the next four chapters go on to describe a variety of practical ways in which support can be delivered. In the meantime, I have made the following points in this chapter:

- The contribution of asynchronous online media is well documented as important for reflection and in supporting a more student-centred approach to study. The respondents to this survey had made use of its potential in the provision of asynchronous computer conferences to extend classroom discussion and offer opportunities for reflection.
- At the same time, face-to-face support has received less attention in the literature, and participants were less overt in the reasons for its use although they were clear about the benefits.
- Synchronous online tools provide alternatives to face-to-face sessions, although they are often problematic for a variety of reasons.
- If blended strategies are to involve a conscious attempt to include both asynchronous and face-to-face or online synchronous contact, we need to know more about the potential contribution of synchronous contact and the influence which asynchronous and synchronous study have on each other.

RESOURCES

Collis, B. (1998) New didactics for university instruction: Why and how? *Computers and Education* **31**, pp. 373–393.

Donnelly, R. (2004) Investigating the effectiveness of teaching online learning in a problem based learning online environment. In Savin-Baden, M. and Wilkie, K. (eds) *Challenging Research into Problem Based Learning.* (Buckingham; OU Press).

Miller, C., Jones, P., Packham, G. and Thomas, B. (2004) A viable solution: The case for blended delivery on an online learning programme. Proceedings of the 4th Networked Learning Conference, Sheffield.

Simpson, O. (2000) *Supporting Students in Open and Distance Learning.* (London, Kogan Page).

PART II

ONLINE TUTORING

CHAPTER 6

SUPPORTING STUDENTS USING ASYNCHRONOUS MEDIA

Email and computer conferences offer a variety of options for tutor- mediated support, which may be used either as a formal part of the course or as an informal adjunct. This chapter discusses the options for supporting individuals and groups, with a focus on the purpose of intervention and the expectations on students and tutors. For illustration, I have drawn on practical examples of conferencing at the Open University (UK), collected from the SOLACE project, in addition to the experiences contributed from other institutions in the blended learning survey, and a variety of 'bright ideas' contributed by tutors.

SUPPORTING THE INDIVIDUAL: EMAIL

Email is widely in use for communication between tutors and individual students, and is particularly common for *informal*, unplanned exchanges, often initiated by the students themselves. Support is given on demand at the point of need, and it is likely to help and support the learning of those who recognise when they need help and assistance. It may be less helpful to those who, for whatever reason, do not realise when they need assistance. In terms of expectations, students should be aware that the support is available; and the role of the tutor might be to reply within an agreed response time.

Email is also used for *formal* assessment-framed support, where the tutor communicates prompt and individualised feedback on assignments in preparation or on work recently completed. In this case the support is given to all students in the group, rather than just those who request it. The use of email, rather than paper-based comments offers potential for more interactivity, and may lead to an ongoing dialogue with students and a sense of connectedness. The electronic medium allows for the use of word processing features such as tracking changes and inserting comments, so that detailed comments could be made on specific parts of the written work, and regularly used comments may be copied from one script to the next. The expectations are that all students will submit work, and the tutor will respond within an agreed timeframe.

MODELS OF CONFERENCING

Much has been written about computer conferencing in the past 15 years, and you might imagine that we know as much as we would wish. Yet, while some practitioners have been highly successful, others remain disillusioned. I have decided to approach this chapter by discussing a variety of models of conferencing, as a way of focusing attention on their purposes and the students they are likely to be able to support. In short, these models of conferencing describe:

- the purpose of the conference;
- the membership, or who it is designed for;
- the expectations which the tutor and students have.

The significance of these models is that they define the tutoring and moderator roles.

There are many ways in which asynchronous conferencing can be used to provide tutor-mediated support within a blended strategy, and there is no reason why a conference might not reflect different models of support at various points in the course. In this section I will describe the approaches which are currently in use, and I will attempt to explain why I believe they work. I hope that they will supply the inspiration to embark on a few innovations yourself.

Some of the ideas which I describe here can be adapted for an email to list for those who do not have access to a VLE or conferencing software but still wish to support their students as a group. The messages will arrive in the list members' regular email inbox, and individual students are responsible for filing, deleting or responding to messages as appropriate. I will indicate where I believe this is a feasible alternative to conferencing. I have divided my comments into those models which cater to a small defined group of students and those which cater for plenary work, since they differ in many important ways. When conferencing, size is critical!

SMALL GROUP CONFERENCES

These conferences commonly have a constant membership of students, who are identifiable individuals to the tutor. These characteristics define the ways in which the conference is used, and the expectation is that the moderator will be concerned with the progress of all students in the group. I describe here two models of support: 'Assessment-framed activity', and 'Interactive resource'.

Assessment-framed activity

Purpose
The conference acts as a forum for activity which is linked to an assignment. Such a model may be important at certain points in the course, for example at the start, where students may need some encouragement to begin participating, or to develop certain skills (see examples in Chapters 12–14). If it is important to you that all your students undertake the learning activities that you have set, then there is little alternative but to frame those activities within the assessment strategy. Most students will probably join in eventually if there are marks to be gained or lost.

Membership and expectations
The membership of a conference where assessment-framed activity takes place will be constant, as it is assumed that all students in the group will be expected to participate. Such conferences may be small, indeed it is quite common for groups to be as small as four students, particularly where they are working towards a collaborative piece of work; for other activities there may be groups of 20 or so. However, it is impossible to be definitive about group size, because there is a relationship between the number of activities which you set, the duration of the activity, the number of participants in the group and the number of messages which you might expect.

MULTIPLYING THE MESSAGES – AND THE WORKLOAD

Case A

Activities:	3, each requiring 4 message postings
Group size:	20 students
Duration of activity:	1 week
Message base:	minimum 240 messages per week, plus moderator messages

----

Case B

Activities:	2, each requiring 3 message postings
Group size:	30 students
Duration of activity:	2 weeks
Message base:	minimum 90 messages per week, plus moderator messages

It is worth pausing to consider the implications for workload on both the moderator and the students, particularly if the group is expected to read all messages as well as undertake the activities you have set. Indeed, Derounian (2003) describes how assessment-related activity generated a total of 41 173 hits from 112 students (28 groups) in one semester on their VLE.

Several variables here might be adjusted. For example, you could alter the workload and size of conference by reducing the number of activities, or the size of the group, or alternatively the nature of the activities themselves, or the time frame over which activities are to be carried out. All this has implications for the flexibility in study routines which may be restricted by assessment-framed activity.

> On the diploma, the tutor group activity is more directly linked to the assessment; part of their assignment is an assessment of the contributions they have made. We made significant modification to the original presentation, because it really restricted flexibility for students. They had to engage with colleagues on collaborative work over a small window of time, so this was very restrictive. It was an excessive burden on tutors to keep on top of discussions. We have increased the time over which activities can be undertaken, and scaled down the number of activities required. We also capped the proportion of online work which contributed to the assignment. (34, Open Univ., UK)

> In order to stimulate qualitative and profound negotiations, an adequate amount of time should be available to discuss. As the discussions are asynchronous and students are expected to respond to each other, we learned that in this specific setting one week is a too short period for online discussions ... As online communication is totally different from face-to-face communication, the specific goals of the discussion groups should be

adapted. At first, the discussion assignments in the online learning environment were based on the assignments in the face-to-face environment. This implies that students were asked to explore the clinical problem, make a diagnosis and propose for further patient management. However, it appeared that it was hardly possible for students to come to a consensus concerning these three issues within the two-weeks time constraints of the asynchronous discussions. Therefore, it appeared better to focus on more specialised issues and to develop specific assignments for the online environment. This is especially important because of the specific advantages of asynchronous discussion groups, such as extra time to reflect, think and search for extra information before contributing to the discussion. (13, Ghent Univ., Belgium)

Role of the tutor moderator

The fact that online activities are central to the course means that all students in the group are expected to participate. While some may need little encouragement to input messages, the moderator may be engaged in chasing up and encouraging those students who are not active on the conference. They may also be responsible for allocating students to small groups for collaborative work. If discussion is extensive, they may be engaged in summarising, weaving and archiving discussion as appropriate. Finally, they may be concerned with assessing the nature and extent of student contributions.

Interactive resource

Purpose

These conferences can play a valuable role in helping the tutorial group to keep in touch throughout the course, on a more continuous basis than has previously been possible. This is particularly valuable for distance learners who may otherwise suffer from isolation and failing motivation. These conferences may also find application on dual mode courses, to join up distance and campus-based students, so that the two cohorts are on a level footing. It is a model where email to list works well.

The conference or email to list is used for timely notices, topical hints and tips, links to further reading, the agenda of a forthcoming tutorial or comments on assignments. There is no assumption that students will respond or join in discussion, although they may do so occasionally and the conference certainly provides a more interactive environment than would be possible with a letter or printed handout. In fact, on courses at the Open University (UK) where online conferencing is in use, such conferences are emerging as a major channel of communication between the tutor and their group. This model of support provides a valuable role in integrating different elements of a blended strategy, while at the same time realigning tutor expectations on participation.

Membership and expectations

This model is commonly used with a relatively stable group of identifiable individuals, who are expected to visit the conference and read messages. Student participation in this context is not crucial for the viability of the conference, although they are free to respond if they wish.

A similar idea might work with a larger plenary group of students, in which case it would be optional whether they read messages or not.

Role of the tutor moderator

The moderator of such a conference is responsible for posting new items generally in keeping the conference 'live' and of course in responding to queries. They may be engaged in archiving material, and perhaps in keeping handy hints and tips or frequently asked questions or reminders from one year to the next. If the conference is for a group of identifiable individuals, the tutor needs to be concerned that the students in their group have actually read the messages (and some software allows you to track those silent readers); however, active participation by students need not be a pre-requisite. For a plenary group, this would of course be difficult or impossible to enforce.

🔆 BRIGHT IDEAS...

I took over teaching this course half-way through the course when I moved to Scotland and as I had already started using the online student Bulletin for my students in [Europe], I adapted it for the Scottish students.

The original Bulletin had been hard copy, sent by snail mail. The material was good, but it took so long to print, collate and deliver that students often reported that it had arrived after they had had to send their [assignments]. In 2003 I found that all my students in Europe had an email address, so I decided to go 'online'... Initially, I simply used the Bulletin as a form of communication to the students – giving advice on the [assignment], updating issues from the course, and providing some of the materials that I used in tutorials. However, I found that this could be developed in 3 ways:

1. by setting 'tasks' which students could complete and then email me for my 'answers'. I developed some form of interactive communication with students that never came to tutorials;

2. by including website addresses in the Bulletin I could encourage students to look for more resources if they needed them (there is a project in the course and I would like to do more on this in 2004);

3. including student's own material – one student was living in Papua New Guinea, a culture which forms part of the 'Exhibiting Culture' element of the course. He sent me some very interesting and relevant photos, which I could disperse electronically to other students.

(Geraldine Wooley, OU tutor)

💡 BRIGHT IDEAS...

Over several weeks I regularly emailed my student group about the night sky. During this period very bright planets Venus and Jupiter seemed to move closer together, passed and separated. This generated plenty of interest, as students realised they could see the changes from night to night. The night these planets passed each other was cloudy, but people were still able to see the event through the clouds. I received several emails from students about the excitement of watching these planets, and there was lots of discussion at tutorials. This brought to life some of the abstract course material on orbits.
(Dave Edwards, OU tutor)

💡 BRIGHT IDEAS...

Towards the exam of the module the tutor group conference has become very quiet – which I could really understand as there are only 11 students in my group (one of them not interacting at all), the schedule is really tight and – as the majority is German – most of them have language difficulties and therefore need more time. I therefore decided to let them know, that everyone of them is busy, it is nevertheless important to have a look in the tutor group conference regularly and that contributions are highly welcome but not a 'must'. I therefore sent the following message to our conference.

```
'Dear all,

Although nothing is obviously happening in here – due to you being
very busy, I can really understand this! :) – I can see from the last
message's history that ALL of you have read my message and downloaded
the attachments.

I hope and assume that you are coming to manage revision besides being
'serious managers' at work and family members at home! (kind of role
conflict and/or overload here?) I wish you all the best and keep my
fingers crossed for all of you to pass the exam!!!

See you in February then!  Looking forward to meeting you again. :)
Kind regards,
Kate'
```

My students' feedback on our following tutorial has been that they appreciated my style of tutoring and thanked for its effectiveness, openness and understanding.
(Katrin Krzewina, OU tutor)

BRIGHT IDEAS...

I decided that I'd like to get going with some conference discussion basically surrounding an 'Assignment Checklist'. Basically, approx two weeks before each assignment, I leave a conference message in which I firstly remind students of all the basics for reading each question thoroughly, planning out an answer, checking grammar and spelling, taking time to reflect etc. (all the stuff we tell them again and again). I then detail specific points against each question that I feel students should take into account when answering that question. To create these specifics, I revise the question myself as well as refer to the marking guidelines. I would really recommend this method to colleagues teaching online – it really works and students really find it worthwhile.
(Brendan Murphy, OU tutor)

PLENARY CONFERENCES

Support can be delivered to larger groups in a variety of ways using asynchronous conferences. Such plenary conferences may represent the sole channel of support on some courses, and they can be a cost effective approach in terms of tutor time to support large numbers of students. In most cases the conference will support the learning of those students who are interested enough to participate, or at least to lurk and read the messages.

However, while large conferences do provide valuable tuition and peer support and probably excel in terms of their reflective, timely or perhaps interactive qualities, they tend to provide for those students who have the time or confidence to participate. Of course, there is no easy way of identifying those students who may have fallen by the wayside, if that is considered important.

There is some evidence that such conferences are more effective with students who are already confident as self-directed learners, whether because of their stage of academic development or perhaps cultural influences in their educational background. It is probably a case of recognizing the place of this type of support amongst a range of strategies to support our students.

The following three models of conferencing all cater to a variable membership of students. I am going to describe here 'The running commentary'; 'Queries and help'; and 'Informal learning and socialising' with respect to their purposes, membership and the implications for the role of the tutor moderator.

The running commentary

Purpose

A common use of plenary conferences is to provide a running commentary on course issues. Students may discuss their understanding (or lack of it) of course concepts as they are encountered either in lectures or course materials, and to relate these issues to their own experiences, sometimes effectively extending tutorial discussion. The conference provides a platform for students to make sense of course materials, and perhaps to practise writing appropriately within the discipline.

> *As a student I found a main advantage of [plenary] conferencing was that other students often asked the question that I did not yet know I needed to ask!! The tutor liked it as he not only answered the question asked but also gave study hints and answered associated queries that were not asked directly.* (OU student)

> *... a consequence, perhaps unforeseen, of [plenary] conferences is that everything you post reaches an audience of about 90, whether you want it to or not! I have to say also that I first started looking at the student conferences from the relatively self-centred viewpoint of 'what shall I do with them at my own tutorial tomorrow, based on what the articulate ones seem to be saying are the sticking points'.* (OU tutor)

> *... I use an asynchronous communication forum. Distance and on-campus students [100 students, 30 on campus, 70 off campus] use this forum to discuss the material, to ask questions about aspects of the practical exercises and assessable assignment tasks, and to discuss software configuration problems. In a typical teaching session there will be more than 1000 postings to this forum. [This is over a 13–16 week period]. In recent sessions I have divided the forum up into sub-forums relating to specific topics in order to better manage this large volume of messages.* (10, Charles Sturt Univ., Australia)

There are of course many other variations. For example, some courses use plenary conferences for visiting experts to answer questions and orchestrate discussion in their particular field, over a fixed period of perhaps a week. They are also useful in the revision period, to provide much valued support and encouragement before the exam.

⌣̈ BRIGHT IDEAS...

We independently work out solutions of last year's exams. We then exchange and compare files and establish agreed solution files which we then circulate electronically on the conference for the next course presentation. During the revision period, students are working on past papers, but don't know whether what they are doing is correct or not.

The hit rate on FirstClass is about 5% of all students (currently ca. 5000 to 6000 p.a.), but we know that both students and tutors distribute our solutions more widely, so over the four years we have been doing it electronically (previously it was postal requests) a conservative estimate is 1500 – 2000 students. There have been repeated requests for re-posting.

(Margaret McColm and Norman Thomson, OU tutors.)

Membership and expectations

It is common for participation to depend on the appeal and relevance of the discussion to students. This means that the group membership may shift continually, although some students may be enduring enthusiasts. Such groups may have 100 or more participants, and some writers have likened such conferences to a debate on the radio where a few individuals take part but large numbers of listeners benefit. Of course, some students do neither of these things.

Role of the tutor moderator

With the advantage of a large 'critical mass' of students who might participate, the job of sustaining online participation is less problematic than it might otherwise be. However dealing with the sheer volume of messages may become a serious problem both for the moderator and for the students who join the conference.

Duties may involve the management and archiving of large numbers of messages; summarising, weaving and the initiation of new topics; and dealing with inappropriate messages. Such large conferences may lend themselves to team teaching, perhaps engaging an experienced tutor alongside one who is less so, or working a rota system to allow for holidays and time off. Commonly, moderators receive many emails from individual students in addition to their duties with respect to the group, with potentially serious implications for tutor workload.

My mailbox has been bulging with messages from individual students since I started moderating this conference. Students seem to feel they know me, and will use me as the first port of call for anything and everything. (OU tutor)

Queries and help

Purpose
A plenary conference may serve as a helpdesk, where students are free to ask questions by posting their messages, which are answered by an expert. The queries and attendant answers may be archived as FAQs (Frequently Asked Questions), so that they can be used as a reference source by subsequent enquirers. Unfortunately human nature being what it is, students are far more likely to post messages than to check FAQs for problems which have already been answered. Such conferences might be used for technical or course-related support.

Membership and expectations
This model can be effective when operated for large groups of students, although membership is not constant but rather changes with the particular need for information. In fact, it is effectively a support service to the individual unless fellow students read the FAQs.

Role of the tutor moderator
The role of the moderator in this case is to respond promptly to incoming queries and to maintain the conference in good order by filing or archiving similar queries together.

Informal learning and socialising

Purpose
We know that much learning actually takes place beyond the classroom, and that students value the opportunity to discuss their course or future courses or indeed anything else under the sun. The extent to which they wish to do this online and asynchronously may depend on a variety of factors, and in particular the alternatives available to them. After all, students who are based on campus may prefer meeting in a real bar rather than a virtual one. But for those who otherwise may not have the opportunity to meet fellow students, asynchronous conferences are popular and widely in use.

Some tutors find it profitable to join in such discussion themselves from time to time, because it can be used to give a topical flavour to course concepts.

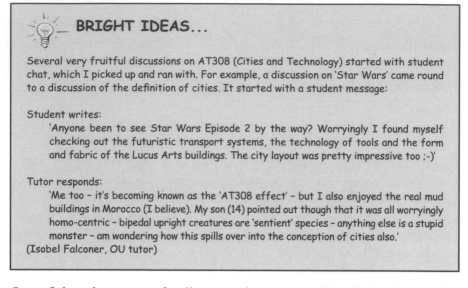

One of the advantages of online asynchronous working is that it provides an opportunity for current students to meet alumni, thus bridging the divide between one course and the next. It can be a popular way for students to discuss the options for choosing new courses.

BRIGHT IDEAS...

I use online for this years' students to chat to last years' students in the first month of the course. This allows them to get a peer's view of the course. At the start of the course students can feel overwhelmed by the amount of computing skills they have to learn for conferencing, electronic submission of assignments and ICT skills. By the middle and end of the course students are usually so positive about it that I felt it would be valuable for some of this enthusiasm to be passed onto new students. I also felt students may feel more able to raise concerns with experienced peers than with myself.

I contacted two of last year's students and asked them if they would run a subconference for this year's students within my tutor group area. We called it 'Old Hands'. I explained the purpose of the conference and welcomes were posted. The two former students were then left to run the group with myself popping in just to read messages. They organised a synchronous 'chat', so the students could experience this facility and respond to queries and concerns. It involved 20 of this year's students and two former students. Messages focussed mainly on reassurance that the course was do-able, tips re peer support and hints on time management.
(Fiona Harkes, OU tutor)

Asynchronous conferences may serve in addition as a platform for any number of hobbies and clubs.

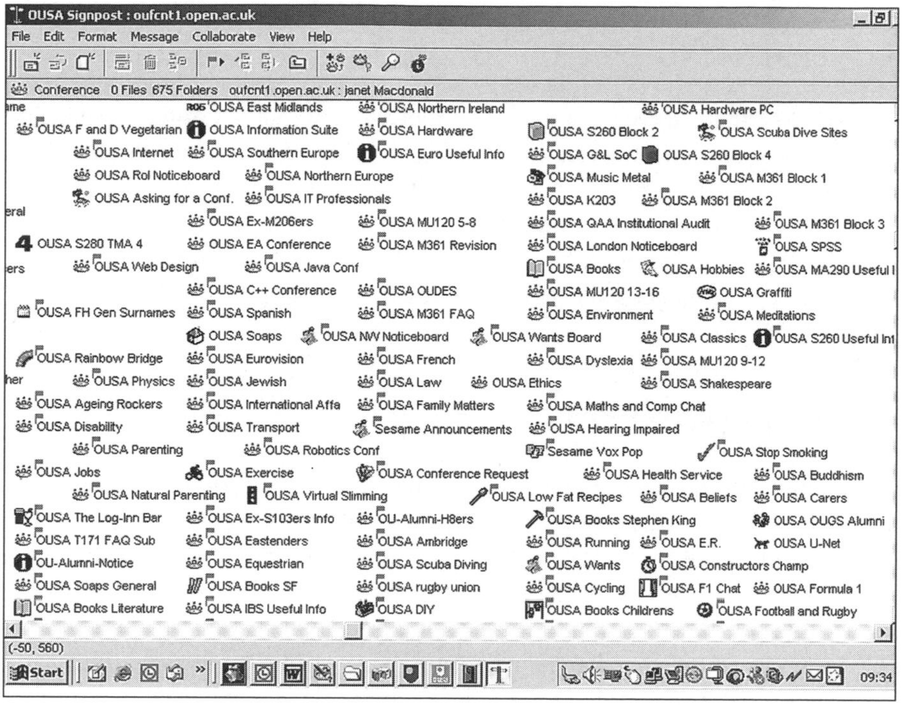

Figure 6.1   **From Startrek to Shakespeare: computer conferencing for socialising. Reproduced with kind permission from the Open University**

Membership

Comments on the membership of plenary conferences apply here – many conferences will have enthusiasts who persist, but commonly the population will shift with the relevance of the topic under discussion, and participation is entirely optional.

Role of the tutor moderator

Membership and participation in such groups is a reflection of student interest in the subject under discussion. If participants veer 'off topic', that is often accepted as an integral, if frustrating, part of such conferences. If such conferences are moderated at all, the moderator may be simply concerned with dealing with inappropriate messages.

SUMMARISING THE OPTIONS FOR COMPUTER CONFERENCING

I have described here a variety of models of computer conferencing, and showed how realistic expectations on the viability of online conferences and moderator roles are linked to an understanding of the purpose and membership. Table 6.1 summarises the options I have discussed here for supporting the group. We use it as the basis of our online training for moderators, since it effectively delineates the responsibilities of moderators for a variety of models of conference.

NOT WORKING WELL?

I have concentrated here on what works, but it would be worth mentioning why so often asynchronous conferencing does not work as well as expected. For example, the models I have listed for a plenary group rely for their success on a critical mass of students who are interested enough to participate. Working on a rough calculation of a third of the population who are active contributors, it is not very surprising if, from a group of 20 students, the six potentially active students find conferencing a little lonely. This is why the two models I have described for small group work do not rely on participation unless that is framed by the assessment. Conversely, you are able to do different types of task with a group whose membership is relatively constant, allowing you to work with identifiable individuals and to be aware of times when they are absent or in difficulty.

Secondly, the success of asynchronous working will depend on what alternatives the students have available to them, and how relatively attractive they are perceived to be. It might be easy to 'sell' the benefits of asynchronous conferencing to a distance student working on an oil rig; but perspectives will be different for campus-based students who otherwise meet each other and their tutors regularly in class or corridor.

Thirdly, some disciplines lend themselves to text based discussion more readily than others. Danchak and Huguet (2004) describe how their discussion board for a course on computer-aided design 'failed miserably':

Table 6.1   Models of computer conferencing

Small Groups Size: c. 4–30 Membership: Constant with identifiable individuals			
Model	**Purpose**	**Moderator Roles**	**Expectations on Participants**
Assessment framed activity	Activity framed by assessment at certain points in course	Identifying and encouraging non-participants; summarising, weaving, archiving	All students must participate actively at crucial times
Interactive resource	Keeping in touch on continuous basis throughout course, with timely notices, topical tips	Posting notices; hints and tips; responding to queries; watching for non-present members	All students must read messages regularly, and may post messages if they wish
Plenary Groups **Size: c. 50–several hundred** **Membership: Variable, according to interest and relevance**			
Model	**Purpose**	**Moderator Roles**	**Expectations on Participants**
Running commentary	Providing a running commentary on course issues as encountered and relating that to personal experience	Summarising; weaving; archiving. Scope for team tutoring	Often the most articulate students post messages. Some just read. Other may not join at all
Visiting 'speaker'	Answering questions and orchestrating discussion over period related to relevant part of course	Responding to queries; posing questions for debate	
Revision	Approaches to revision and exam work; or answers to previous exam questions	Delivering model answers; responding to queries; posing questions for debate	
Queries and helpdesk	Helpdesk for course related or technical support	Responding to queries; archiving; FAQs	
Social	Hobbies and interests, or joining up alumni with current cohort	Probably N/A	

> *... the questions asked had correct answers, even though there could be some variation. After covering the spectrum of reasonable responses, students soon began to say 'I agree with Joe', meaning they agreed with a response posted by another student. What we needed were authentic questions; questions that had no right answer, but caused students to reflect and consider different perspectives ... Doing this in a technology course is often a challenge.* (Danchak and Huguet, 2004, p 206)

Finally, it is important to be realistic in your expectations of your students. Regardless of the medium used, there is some evidence that students may be more likely to take part in tasks which are already familiar to them. Conversely, there may be little mileage in setting online tasks which students commonly experience difficulty with in face-to-face situations, as these authors comment:

> *The point is that many students are simply not very familiar with the activity of discussion even in face-to-face settings, and the provision of text conferencing will not alter that fact. The result is that they are more likely to revert to communications of the type with which they are familiar – information exchange, coordination of collaborative activity, question and answer sessions with teachers – or even not use the conference at all. Attempts by tutors to moderate exchanges and encourage discussion may only succeed in introducing interactions of the Initiation – Response – Evaluation form, common in face-to-face tutorials, i.e. where tutors pose questions to individual students, students respond, and tutors comment on students' responses.* (McAteer et al., 2000)

IN SUMMARY

What implications does all this have for successful conferencing? First of all we need to be clear what we mean by success! It must surely be a situation where the objectives are achieved, whatever they might be, and where the expectations of participation are realistic. Success in online tutoring begins with an understanding of what online tools do well, and under what conditions. My comments are as follows.

Purpose of conference and membership

The size of the conference and the status of the membership, whether constant or variable, will define what you are able to do. Conferences may be set up with various purposes, as we have already discussed. But whatever they are, it certainly helps if the contents of the conference are timely and relevant. The conference needs to look lively.

The moderator

A critical factor for lively participation in a conference is the regular and active engagement of the moderator. The role of moderator, and the jobs which it entails, will depend on the purposes and membership of the conference.

The students

Despite the best laid plans, some students are more likely to participate actively than others, for a variety of reasons. This may change, at different stages in the course, and so we should be wary of attaching labels to them. Students who are familiar with asynchronous conferencing from previous courses are likely to be less anxious about participating. If conferencing is perceived as the norm, they are more likely to accept it. And some groups 'gel' better than others – it varies from one presentation to the next, or from year to year.

As you have seen, computer conferences can be used a variety of ways for tutor-mediated support, and the job of the moderator will vary with the purposes of the conference which they moderate. In Chapter 7, I have included examples of moderator skills which are commonly, although not invariably, in use. You will also find some ideas for activities in Chapters 12 to 14, where they relate to the development of competence in e-learning and blended learning.

RESOURCES

Danchak, M. M. and Huguet, M.P. (2004) Designing for the changing role of the instructor in blended learning. *IEEE Transactions on Professional Communication* **47** (3) pp. 200–210.

Derounian, J. (2003) *LEAP (Learning Environments and Pedagogy) Case Study 11*. Higher Education Academy. http://www.heacademy.ac.uk/Leap. htm, (accessed 29th Apr 2005).

McAteer, E., Tolmie, A., Crook, C., McLeod, H. (2000) *Learning Networks: Communication Skills*. Final report to the Joint Information Systems Committee www.gla.ac.uk/lncs (accessed 26th May 2005).

CHAPTER 7

HANDY TECHNIQUES FOR MODERATORS:
ONLINE CONFERENCES

I described in Chapter 6 how the job of the moderator will vary with the purpose of the conference which they moderate and its membership. In this chapter, I have included examples of moderator skills which are commonly, although not invariably, in use in many conferences. A great deal has already been written in this area; please see the 'Resources' section at the end of this chapter if you want to read further.

Running a conference is really not so far removed from many familiar activities at university or college, whether that is running a tutorial, keeping students up to date with course events or helping with ad hoc problems. You probably already have the skills: the trick is to use them effectively in a new environment.

CONFERENCE AIMS AND OBJECTIVES

It is helpful to let participants know what the purposes of the conference are, and, where relevant, your expectations of their participation, over what timescale, and your own likely contributions and response times.

Introductions and setting the scene

In some conferences, the moderator will be responsible for introducing themselves to the group, and in encouraging group members to 'meet' each other online. This is really not too different from face-to-face introductions with a group, although you might need to work a little harder because participants cannot see or hear each other. There is a wide variety of icebreaker activities which can be used, and you will find some examples in the box below.

BRIGHT IDEAS...

The hardest thing is to get people to join in for the first time. I tend to use my picture in my introductory message to give the students some idea of who they are dealing with – failing that, they might get a laugh! I also encourage them to send in a mugshot of themselves for the rogues' gallery.

I like to make the first icebreaker light-hearted and, out of all the ones tried, the 'guess my truth' brings in the most response. The students submit a message and tell two untruths and one truth. The untruths are generally funny and this provides a non-threatening entry into cyber world. The complicated ones tend to put the students off.
(Maggie Barrowman, OU tutor)

In a conference I would ask students to relate an amusing, weird or memorable event that arose because they were an OU student. The concentration on 'OU student' reinforces identity with the university and sharing incidents helps forge a group identity. Two things normally missing from conferencing – anecdote and humour.
(Graham McMaster, OU tutor)

My icebreaker is usually focused on the particular course and I ask the students to share two issues with the group and point out that I will be the first to share my two issues with them:
1.   What is your great excitement in doing this course?
2.   What is your worry?
(Tony Kelly, OU tutor)

I like the idea of a more numerate type of icebreaker for students on mathematics and computing courses who may feel more at home discussing such matters. I would use something such as: '3 3 5 4 4 3 5 5 4 3 … what comes next?'
(Chris Woodford, OU tutor)

Students can feel apprehensive about any icebreaker activity that involves the course, so I tend to keep mine very general or unrelated to either the course or personal preferences. One that has been successful both online and FTF is as follows:

Post a grid of numbers (either 3 × 3 or 4 × 4. For example,
```
 1   3   5
 4   8   12
11  15  9
```

Then ask the students which is the odd one out and why. A variety of answers will be given. The actual answer is whatever number you decide – because it is the only one on a menu with rice as opposed to noodles. As long as this isn't strung out too long it usually raises a laugh and seems to relax people.
(Julie Robson, OU tutor)

Is there a trivial claim to fame that you are willing to own up to?
'My first serious girlfriend became an opera singer and regularly sang at Covent Garden and her daughter is one of the 'Opera Babes'.'
'Mine is that I exchange Christmas cards with a colleague who lives next door to Tony Blair's aunty!'
(Peter Neal and Anne Campbell, OU tutors)

Archiving

Archiving simply means that you are responsible for the electronic filing of messages which relate to a particular topic, so that users of the conference can refer to them more readily. This is particularly important where plenary discussion conferences have a shifting population of students, who may arrive halfway through the discussion and are otherwise swamped by unread messages.

Weaving

Weaving is a term used to describe the facilitation of an online discussion, much as a tutor might do in a face-to-face tutorial. It involves picking up threads contributed by participants and moving the discussion on. See the example in the box below.

Summarising

Summarising is a similar skill to weaving and, like weaving, it might be more appropriate to some subject areas than others. It simply means that the moderator will draw together an overview of what has been contributed on the conference, perhaps towards the end of the discussion period. The summary serves to check that the discussion as recorded actually reflects the views of participants, and it can very often stimulate further contributions.

Threading

In conferences with lively discussions it can often be the case that large numbers of messages have a subject line which bears little relation to the content of the message. This happens when participants contribute to the conference by hitting 'reply' to the last message. You could start a new thread, with an appropriate heading.

Managing online interactions

In some conferences it will be important that all students participate, in which case the moderator will be responsible for ensuring that they do. This will certainly require tact and diplomacy, and may well be a case for contacting students individually in order to discuss the reasons for non-appearance on the conference. In other conferences, it will be important that students read your messages, and some software allows you to track the readership of messages. Again, you may need to contact students individually if they have not been on the conference.

AN ILLUSTRATION OF WEAVING IN AN ASYNCHRONOUS DISCUSSION

Tutor Sophie opens the debate:
From your experiences with conferencing, I wonder if you could comment on the following statement? 'Online conferencing can be unnerving, and often unpredictable as a way of supporting students.'

Jane writes:
As a participant, I wonder how many students would – like me – feel quite overwhelmed by it? On the one hand, it is great when you think you can communicate to all these people – and possibly get responses – but on the other hand it is intimidating to 'speak' to a group of relatively anonymous people, who might also have lots more experience at online conferencing. I think that in F2F and to some extent even in telephone conferencing you can, as a tutor, gauge how your students are feeling. Is this possible in online conferencing?

Tutor Sophie (weaving):
Jane makes a very valid point about the anxieties associated with conferencing. But I wonder if you others feel that this continues to be a serious hurdle once students are familiar with the medium?

Patsy writes:
I suppose that you could argue that any form of human exchange, especially learning-related, can be 'unnerving and unpredictable' and some learning theorists like Carl Rogers would probably encourage that. Once online learners know the rules, and they need them, because invisible dialogue does seem to provoke more 'flaming' than face-to-face discussion, then we can expect more predictable behaviours.

Peter writes:
Students often perceive themselves as 'intellectual islands' that must stand alone when it comes to assignments and other such tasks. This may be because many of our learners were brought up in learning situations that were not designed for much interaction (desks in rows facing the front) except with the teacher.

Tutor Sophie (weaving):
Well, Patsy and Peter's points make me suspect that maybe the hurdle for our students is not so much related to online conferencing as it is to the prospect of group work of any kind? What do others think?

Frances writes:
I think that maybe as tutors we are sometimes less sensitive than we might be to students' real motivations. Whereas the able students enrol with enthusiasm, sparked by genuine interest in the underlying subject matter, the rest are often there primarily to obtain a qualification ... This may sound a bit cynical, but I think that student motives are often more mixed than we as teachers, and ipso facto subject enthusiasts, like to admit.

A SUMMARY OF AN ASYNCHRONOUS DISCUSSION

Tutor Sophie writes:
You've raised a number of important issues related to supporting students using online conferencing:

- students are often anxious about exchanging views with people they don't know, and particularly in an unfamiliar medium;
- messages can be misleading and upsetting, in the absence of visual cues;
- many of our students are not used to working with the group;
- some students may be more oriented towards studying for their qualification, and be less inclined to spend time in debating with fellow students.

Does this represent your views? Maybe you have points you would like to add?

Email and conference messages are famous as a medium for misunderstandings, and therefore it is important for all participants to write clear messages with a friendly tone. Messages should not be longer than a screen and the subject line should be informative. Where students forget these simple rules and offend others, it will be the moderator's job to contact the offender or, in extreme cases, to withdraw the offending message.

Managing your own time

Some conference aims can be very demanding of tutor time, and keeping up with the messages can be addictive. It is helpful to have a strategy for your own time management, including how often you intend to check the conference, and the time delay within which you expect to respond to messages or alternatively wait for fellow students to reply. You may also wish to consider how you will deal with emails that are addressed to you, instead of to the conference. Remember that online moderating need not be a solitary occupation and you might be able to moderate jointly with a fellow tutor. Let your students know how you intend to work, and do not forget to tell them if you are likely to be away from the conference for any significant period.

☀ BRIGHT IDEAS...

When a student asks a question directly to my mailbox I always reply directly to their mailbox.

However, I often copy both the question (suitably anonymatised) and the answer into the tutor group's conference so everyone can share the information. This also encourages other students to ask 'obvious' questions.

Early in a course I always reply quickly to students' questions in the tutor group. As the course progresses I increase the reply delay to give other students a chance to reply.

(Dave Horan, OU tutor)

RESOURCES

Collins, M. and Berge, Z. (1996) Facilitating interaction in computer-mediated online courses. http://www.emoderators.com/moderators/flcc.html (accessed 25 May 2005).

McAteer, E., Tolmie, A., Crook, C. and McLeod, H. (2000) *Learning Networks: Communication skills.* Final report to the Joint Information Systems Committee; see www.gla.ac.uk/lncs.

Salmon, G. (2000) *E-moderating: The key to teaching and learning online* (London, Kogan Page).

Salmon, G. (2002) *Etivities. The key to active online learning* (London, Kogan Page).

CHAPTER 8

SUPPORTING STUDENTS USING SYNCHRONOUS MEDIA

While the role of online conferencing is generally accepted as a key part of blended learning, the contribution of face-to-face or online synchronous support has received rather less attention, as I described in Chapter 5. We know that face-to-face tutorials can have many benefits for student learning. However, given that many of the roles traditionally attributed to face-to-face tutorials can be realised asynchronously and online, what is special about synchronous support and how should we be using it? I will address this challenging question by describing a variety of models of support that can be deployed using synchronous media, together with the implications for choice of an appropriate tool.

For illustrations, I have drawn on the experiences of those contributing to the blended learning survey, as well as on examples of current practice at the Open University (UK). I am particularly grateful to Sylvia Warnecke and the Languages, Maths and Computing tutors at the Open University in Scotland, who have contributed greatly to my understanding of differences in approaches to supporting students in their three very different disciplines, through a project on synchronous tuition in which we were recently engaged.

WHAT TOOLS ARE AVAILABLE?

The simplest and probably most universally accessible tool for synchronous support is the telephone. Not only does it remain in regular use for contact with individual distance students, it can also be used to support small groups using an audio conference bridge. It would be foolish to ignore its merits.

Beyond this is a bewildering array of online tools. Synchronous support is unlike asynchronous online support, which, regardless of the platform, involves text-based communication with individuals or a group and the sharing of documents or other files. It encompasses a much more diversified field because the various tools have a wide range of functionalities, with different potential roles for supporting learners. While some tools rely solely on text for communication, others make use of audio or video together with endless permutations of shared workspaces, concept maps, break-out rooms, file sharing and so on. I have listed some of the common functions in Table 8.1.

Table 8.1   The functions of synchronous tools

Synchronous functions	Comment
Audio	Might involve use of landline or mobile telephones or audio via the Internet. May be one-to-one, or many-to-many. Voicemail adds some flexibility for notices to group
Text chat	Text-based messaging one-to-one or between members of a group, either between mobiles or using the Internet. The transcript can often be saved and archived for reference
Whiteboard	A shared space, which might be used for pictures, text or diagrams, just like a flip chart. In some applications, any member of the group can draw or modify the material. A variation is the concept map, which can be used for illustrating relationships in various ways
Break-out rooms	Virtual spaces into which students can be divided into sub-groups for work on a particular topic, analogous to forming sub-groups in a classroom
Application sharing	The option to share or demonstrate the use of programs such as spreadsheets or databases with the group. Students may either be able to interact with the programs, or simply to view them
Synchronised web browsing	Allows group visits to websites for demonstration or the pursuit of additional resources
Polls, feedback, hand-raising	Yes/No or multiple-choice buttons used at regular intervals allow you to establish that all students are following the discussion. Hand-raising button allows for turn taking in audio contributions
Video	Video many-to-many, or one-to-many, commonly used in purpose-built videoconference suites where there is a reliable broadband connection. Desktop videoconferencing may be limited because of lack of access to broadband for many students

Many of these tools can be used in combination with each other, providing a richer learning environment. Even so, you might like to pause and compare the functionality of face-to-face meetings with these tools. With the combination of audio and visual contact, white/blackboard, file sharing and break-out rooms, a shy smile and some lukewarm coffee, face-to-face meetings are hard to beat.

Indeed, the acceptability of a particular tool for supporting learners will depend on the environment. You will probably consider using it if that represents a better way of keeping in contact and supporting students than the alternatives. A synchronous tool may offer options which are not possible in a face-to-face environment. On the other hand, if there is an opportunity for students to meet in a classroom it may not be worth bothering with technology.

> *Meetings in real time are not used via the chat as the participants wish to see each other.* (44, Univ. Lulea, Sweden)

> *We have asked the students if they felt that the first meeting was unnecessary, but only one out of 48 answered yes. The other students appreciated the meeting and found it necessary; some of them also said that they would have appreciated one more physical meeting. This was of personal reasons. During their joint effort they became close friends and wanted to see each other again.* (1, Bergen Univ. College, Norway)

Where face-to-face meetings are simply not practical, as is the case for many distance students, then the use of synchronous tools becomes more acceptable, and the task is to choose a tool which meets your objectives, or at least some of them.

At the same time, a variety of constraints have to be faced when using synchronous tools: the small size of group which can be supported, or the existence of firewalls which may disrupt the sessions particularly where students are using computers at work. If students are working from home with less than optimal computing equipment or unreliable dial-up lines, synchronous tools may not work well. Sometimes it is wise to offer alternatives.

Of course, no sophisticated technology in the world can overcome the fact that distance students may find it difficult or impossible to meet at the same time as the rest of the group. One way to overcome this is to offer formal support to individual students rather than to the group, and perhaps to target those most likely to be in need of motivation and encouragement.

MODELS OF SYNCHRONOUS SUPPORT

The closer a synchronous tool is in functionality to a face-to-face encounter, the more one is tempted to see its potential as a direct replacement for the traditional face-to-face tutorial. But how justifiable is this assumption? With the use of new technologies, the boundaries are dissolving between what we recognise as formal or informal support, as we discover new ways to support students that are not exact equivalents of previous practice. Maybe some of the support traditionally delivered through assignment feedback can be delivered in other ways to the group, or perhaps some of the burden of tutorial support is carried through online asynchronous or synchronous student peer communities, where previously it was the exclusive responsibility of the tutor. Some support that might have taken place in informal moments during tutorials now happens in emails with individuals. The use of synchronous tools rather than a classroom means that one is no longer tied to a particular geographical location, or indeed to a particular tutor, and team teaching becomes feasible. And the availability of asynchronous support in conferences might mean that functions traditionally attributed to tutorials, such as help with forthcoming assignments, are no longer appropriate. The upshot is that the roles which a tutorial filled in the past are unlikely to be the same as the roles it might fulfil in the future.

Although the term 'tutorial' is in common usage, even in an online context, we probably all have very different ideas about what goes on in one, and what tutorials are for. Such understanding might vary with the discipline. For all these reasons, I am not going to write about 'running tutorials' using synchronous tools, but rather concentrate on a variety of models of support. I intend to use these models in the same way as I did in Chapter 6, as a reflection of the aims and objectives of the session, and of its likely membership. I have been guided by the observations made on synchronous support in the blended learning survey: that such sessions can be particularly useful for community building and socialising, for brainstorming and decision making, and for the pacing of studies. In addition, in the SOLACE project tutors valued affective, dialogic or focusing qualities in intervention, all of which are probably easier to achieve synchronously than asynchronously.

One important difference between synchronous and asynchronous support is that in a synchronous session it is entirely possible to cover a range of objectives, and to support the needs of the individual as well as the group. I make no claim to be comprehensive in my choice of models, but I believe this approach is useful in defining a role for synchronous support within a blended strategy and in illustrating how that might influence the choice of a particular tool. I hope it at least provides you with the opportunity to test my ideas against your own experiences.

Assessment-framed activity

However exciting the tool it is simply not realistic to imagine that all your students will participate in a synchronous session unless that activity is framed within the assessment strategy. If the session is viewed as a central part of the course objectives and something in which all students should take part, then there is a good argument for integrating such activity with the assessment strategy. I maintain that the central importance of designing elements of the course so that they are aligned with the objectives and assessment of the course is as true for synchronous support as it is for asynchronous. In this case, the membership and expectation of participation will apply to all students.

Where it is important for students to meet in the initial stages of a project, a synchronous session can fill an important role. We know from the case studies described in Chapter 5 that such meetings can be useful for brainstorming ideas and reaching consensus on procedural matters. In fact, one of the often repeated drawbacks of asynchronous interaction is the difficulty in making decisions. You can probably draw on your own experience of email exchanges that extend over days, straining overloaded mailboxes. Translated into a telephone call, the same topics take five minutes to resolve. The same principle applies to collaborative study.

It may also be appropriate to meet at the end of a course for final presentations. Such practice is currently common among those who use face-to-face meetings, but it could also be feasible using synchronous tools.

What are the implications for choice of tools? For collaborative work, given that part of this process revolves around learning to work with unfamiliar fellow students, you might decide that it was important to have audio, so that students could at least hear each other's voices and gain some impression of individual differences. Audio could also be important for its spontaneity in supporting the generation of new ideas. At the same time, a whiteboard or text facility might be useful for sharing a written record of the discussion, and break-out rooms could allow for small group work. For final presentations, it might be important to have a shared whiteboard for visual aids, supplemented with text or audio for explanations or discussion.

Role of the tutor moderator
In such cases, support takes place in a formally constituted group of identifiable individuals. The tutor moderator may be engaged in chasing up and encouraging those students who are less active. For collaborative work, they may need to allocate students into sub-groups or to organise a transcript as a record of any decisions made.

Practising skills

In some courses the tutor-mediated practice of a particular skill is an objective which can be met in a synchronous session. Of course, the extent to which the use of a synchronous tool is an adequate replacement for a face-to-face session will depend on the skill in question: if your students were learning the motor skills associated with hairdressing, or even practising interpersonal skills, it might not be appropriate. On the other hand, on a course where the practice of online learning was part of the objectives, you might wish students to gain experience of using the synchronous tool itself.

The membership of such sessions might vary with levels of interest or the stage in the course, and sessions could be run according to demand on a 'fill up and go' system.

The choice of synchronous tool will depend on the skill to be learnt. For example, in languages teaching, where great importance is placed on encouraging students to practise their speaking skills with fellow students, audio is central to the objectives of the session. There may also be clear advantages to being able to share visual information, so that students can practise their descriptive skills; and they might wish to do so in pairs or small groups, in which case break-out rooms are desirable.

Role of the tutor moderator
The moderator will be responsible for advertising skills practice in conjunction with other moderators and responding to demand. They will have devised appropriate activities, and supply feedback and encouragement as appropriate.

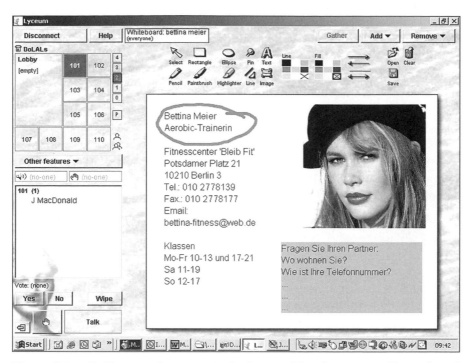

Figure 8.1   Online synchronous tools for teaching languages. Reproduced with kind permission from the Open University (UK)

This tool allows for sophisticated use of whiteboards, audio and break-out rooms to support course objectives: in this case, speaking German. The screen in Figure 8.1 is for the following exercise:

1. The group of students are allocated to two break-out rooms. Each contains a different picture, which they are required to study and discuss.
2. Each student is then paired with a partner from the other room and allocated to their own break-out room.
3. Each student has to describe to their partner (in German) what their picture contained.
4. The whole group re-gathers in a plenary session, where each student reports on their partner's description.

Explaining difficult concepts

Where particular parts of the course are difficult for students to understand, there is a case for providing them with an opportunity to undertake relevant activities to reinforce concepts or to discuss their understanding, supported by the tutor. This activity is often supplemented by the use of online tools and resources, such as formative assessment packages, quizzes or simulations, as a precursor to tutor-mediated support. For example, Danchak and Huguet

(2004) describe how students completed an online quiz with the instructor 'looking over their shoulder'. If the student did the quiz well, the tutors could send a congratulatory message. If they got some answers wrong, then the tutor could establish whether they understood why their answers were incorrect. In other words, synchronous support can be appropriate in order to provide encouragement and to engage students in a dialogue until it is clear that they have understood the concept.

The membership of such a session might be defined by the interest of any students who opt to join in; or it could be offered to particular individuals identified by the tutor as in need of help. It may often be a relatively ad hoc session, and therefore any complicated planning with a combination of synchronous tools is less appropriate.

A choice of synchronous tool will be influenced by the need to cope with the student's anxiety associated with trying to understand a difficult concept, and audio dialogue may be appropriate in contributing reassurance. There are often other discipline-related needs. For example, problem solving in maths may require students to look at exemplars, observe the development of a solution or share software. I am unconvinced of the potential of text chat alone for this kind of support to a group: the medium is simply too anarchic for constructive dialogue because of the way in which sentences are generally broken up into parts, and it also provides little in the way of cues to the tutor to indicate how much students really understand. However, it has some application in supporting individual students, and in the example below it has been used in conjunction with application sharing.

Role of the tutor moderator
The moderator may be responsible for identifying those students most in need of help. They may be responsible for planning exercises, providing resources and illustrations and visual materials, and may maintain an archive of commonly encountered problems from one course presentation to the next.

Induction, informal learning and socialising

Synchronous tools are sometimes used to replace the informal chat which might otherwise take place in the corridor on the way to lectures, or over a cup of coffee. It is the kind of exchange which makes working with people easier because you begin to see them as individuals.

BRIGHT IDEAS...

I have been using online synchronous tutorials since 1999. The sotfware provides a whiteboard for me (or my students, if I invite them) to draw on, a text chat interface for us all to write into, and the facility to share the software on my computer (i.e. the course software) so that I can demonstrate concepts. The single drawback is that the software only supports speech between two users – this is fine for a special session, but for a tutor group we all have to use the text interface, which certainly slows down the interaction (and makes your typing improve!).

This has included a special session with a student in Thurso who I identified, early in the course, as having difficulty with the course concepts – specifically writing computer code. Having agreed that one or the other of us would spend an inordinate amount of time travelling to achieve a face-to-face special session, we settled on a 1.5 hour one-to-one session online. We started off using speech, which became problematic because my student was using a microphone and speakers which caused feedback (I could hear my own voice a couple of heartbeats out of sync, which is very disconcerting). So we went onto text with the fallback of speech where needed – this worked well. During the session I shared my Learning Book (the course software), and demonstrated how I would write some simple code to achieve a certain objective. I then asked the student if he would like to try some – 'yes please' came the eager reply. Passing control of the software across to the student, I watched and occasionally spoke as he managed to write some working code which he could then run within my Learning Book. Suffice to say, this special session helped the student overcome his difficulties with code writing, and I'm sure it helped him to persevere and achieve his eventual Grade 2 for the course.
(Clive Buckland, OU tutor)

In terms of membership, students may maintain this contact with a fairly restricted group of familiar colleagues, although braver souls may chat with whoever is online at the time. The medium is particularly popular with young students. Where community building is a part of course induction, it may be desirable for all students to be involved.

For a choice of tools, text chat or instant messaging is often used by students to keep in touch with each other, as a channel for peer support, and as a way of maintaining motivation to study. For more formally constituted sessions, the sense of presence which people get from a text chat 'conversation' can be reproduced using asynchronous conferencing within a limited time frame by setting a two-hour time slot for input. The discussion can benefit from the use of threading and the facility to archive by topic. The following example describes the use of text chat at the start of a course on climatology for a class of 18-year-olds. Not only did the session provide an introduction to the people on the course, it served as an introduction to the technology of logging on and posting messages.

> *The chat group was a valuable experience because it allowed external tutors, who had not met the students in face-to-face classes, to get to know their designated groups and to begin to form some impression of individual students – which student logged on regularly, how they interacted with each other online – for example 'slanging' matches between the young men, teasing a female student about her height, discussing what they would do in their spare time and generally 'chatting', often using abbreviations used for cell-phone text messages in addition to written forms of the local dialect. Chats with tutors were usually more deferential, particularly with an unknown foreign tutor ... often centred round the students' reactions to the course. (*Ardus and Fabi, 2003; 3, Istituto Tecnico Agrario Statale, Italy)

Role of the tutor moderator

If socialising forms part of the initial induction stages of the course, then the moderator will be engaged in advertising use of the session and encouraging participants to join in and introduce themselves. This could involve icebreakers or similar activities. Beyond that, such exchanges are largely unmoderated.

Short queries

On certain courses, particularly those which may engage students in problem solving or numerical calculation, tutors may arrange regular question-and-answer sessions. Such sessions may be advertised as available to any students on the course with queries, and so can cater for a shifting population of students who vary with the current query and its topical relevance.

Text chat is commonly used in this context, and I imagine it might work best in subjects where both queries and their answers are short. At the Open University library, an application of text chat for short queries is the 'Librarians On Call' service, where it is deployed as a way of dealing with incoming queries from staff and students (see Figure 8.2).

> *Webchat is excellent for short, quick queries. It enables us to help direct users to the page of the Open Library website or an external website that will answer their question quickly and easily. It isn't the ideal medium for long, complex queries and, in those cases, we will take contact details for a user and get back to them asap. Users, however, value the instant response and have the advantage of knowing their query is being dealt with, which is less obvious with email queries.* (OU library staff member)

Role of the tutor moderator

The moderator will be responsible for being available at agreed times, and responding promptly to any queries posted. They may maintain an archive of frequently asked questions and the answers.

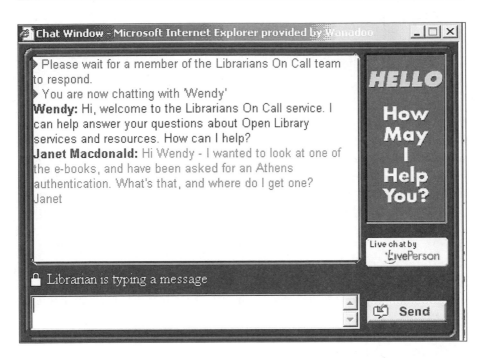

Figure 8.2 **Librarians On Call. The library runs a help service for enquirers using text chat. Reproduced with kind permission from the Open University**

Timely reminders

There is potential for using synchronous tools to issue timely notices and reminders to students, such as 'Don't forget to come to the next tutorial' or 'Remember the date for the next assignment'. Such a strategy might work with a defined group of known individuals or perhaps even a large group of unknown individuals. Of course the success of using a technology like short message service (SMS) messaging depends on having a critical mass of students with mobile phones and, furthermore, phones that are continually switched on.

For really short bulletins, SMS text messages are probably a useful tool in this context. For longer bulletins with topical hints and tips or perhaps the agenda for the next tutorial, voicemail can be used. It fulfils a similar model of support to that described for the interactive resource using computer conferences or email to list, but it has a greater sense of urgency.

Role of the tutor moderator
The moderator will be responsible for issuing bulletins and responding to related queries as they arrive.

Opinion polls

Polls can add a sense of topicality to a course by encouraging students to contribute their views on a course topic. That might be particularly relevant where some course topic was exemplified by current events. Students might be asked to respond to a simple Yes/No question using email or text, or more detailed responses might be accommodated using blogs. Such an activity could be advertised to all students as an opportunity which some might find attractive and others not.

Role of the tutor moderator
The moderator will be responsible for inviting students to respond to the poll, and perhaps for collating the results, or otherwise making them available to all students.

Motivation and milestones

It has often been remarked how useful synchronous events can be to provide motivation and a goal to work towards, and as an opportunity for tutors to establish how their students are coping with the course. Such support might take place with the group, but can also be very effective with individual students. For example, the Open University (UK) runs a series of access courses designed to encourage students with little previous educational experience into study. On these courses, individual support delivered by telephone has been highly effective in promoting student confidence and encouraging retention (Gaskell and Mills, 2004).

The choice of an appropriate tool might be a question of something which is readily accessible and would support the affective elements of support. In this context, audio is particularly helpful in conveying encouragement and a whiteboard might be useful for illustrating explanations.

Role of the tutor moderator
The tutor moderator will be responsible for contacting students at agreed intervals and for providing a responsive and motivating approach to support.

IN SUMMARY

One of the most exciting things about synchronous tutor-mediated support is that the availability of synchronous tools challenges us to reflect on areas of practice which have long been familiar, and for which the tutor's expertise has been implicit. In particular, we have to think about the contribution of the synchronous component in blended learning, where some of the traditionally accepted benefits of tutorials may be taking place in other ways. This is an area where our knowledge and understanding are still fragmented. It is also an aspect which may not be relevant at all to course designers who are able to make use of face-to-face sessions.

In the next chapter, I continue this theme by describing practical tips for using a variety of synchronous tools. I have made the following points in this chapter:

*   Synchronous tools have a wide variety of functionalities with a spectrum of capacities to support different aspects of learning. Many of them can be used together in one session.
*   All these tools support small groups, and most will have technical and access limitations for both students and tutors.
*   They can be used to meet a variety of learning objectives to meet the needs of either a group of identifiable individuals or a plenary group.
*   Any synchronous activity that is central to the course will still need to be framed by the assessment.

RESOURCES

Ardus, J. and Fabi, F. (2003) 'A raga'. Scuola Online 2003: E-learning in a rural community: a tutor's view. http://www.sol.celleno.it/raga.htm (accessed 13 January 2005).

Danchak, M.M. and Huguet, M.P. (2004) Designing for the changing role of the instructor in blended learning. *IEEE Transactions of Professional Communication* **47** (3), pp. 200–210.

Gaskell, A. and Mills, R. (2004) Supporting students by telephone: a technology for the future of student support? http://www.change.co.nz/docs/eden/Gaskell.pdf (accessed 8 October 2004).

CHAPTER 9

HANDY TECHNIQUES FOR MODERATORS:
ONLINE SYNCHRONOUS SESSIONS

I have gathered here some tips for good practice in supporting students using a variety of online synchronous tools. You will see that there are general principles that apply to all these tools and tips that apply to particular tools. Of course, you may very well be employing more than one tool at a time in your session.

I am indebted to a number of colleagues at the Open University (UK) for their invaluable contributions to good practice in this area: these include Anne Gaskell and co-authors of the Supporting Students by Telephone toolkit, because many of the good practice guidelines for telephone tuition which they have collected apply equally well to other synchronous tools. I am also grateful to Sylvia Warnecke and the Languages and Maths tutors at the Open University in Scotland, for their contribution to good practice guidelines in using audiographics tools. See the 'Resources' section at the end of this chapter for more details.

GENERAL TECHNIQUES

Preparation

Expect to accommodate a group of no more than six students, although larger groups can work if you have break-out rooms. In general, the larger the group, the more formal the session and the more preparation you will need to do. Circulate your students beforehand, so that they are aware of what to expect. You might include the learning objectives and an agenda, with timings and perhaps some detail about the activities, if they require preparation. Plan for shorter activities than you would for face-to-face work. Allow for no more than an hour's session overall.

Think about your choice of tool. The use of several tools at a time will allow you to create a richer learning environment, but you will certainly end up with a more formal session. If you use one tool on its own, then you can probably afford to be more informal and ad hoc. Some tools are more appropriate to particular learning objectives, as discussed in Chapter 8.

Plan for activities that will engage students and encourage them to communicate with each other. Avoid lecturing – that can be mind-numbing. Break up your sessions with small group work in break-out rooms if you have them. Alternatively, plan to interrupt your session for periods of individual reflection, and then reconnect after an agreed time.

On the day, ensure that you will not be disturbed, if necessary with a sign on the door. Ask your students to join early if the technology is unfamiliar, or run an induction session simply to introduce the tools. Students will not be interested in other learning outcomes you may have in mind until they are competent with the software. Make sure they learn to be confident in using the tools, so that if you 'disappear' because of some technical glitch, they can continue without you. They also need to know what to do if the technology fails for them.

During the session

Have a strategy for welcoming students. You might decide that the first five minutes will be a period for exchanging news and settling in. You might put a welcome message on a whiteboard if you have one.

Decide how you will greet latecomers. If you are only using one tool, there is no option but to stop and review the proceedings so far when students arrive late. When using several tools, there is scope for reserving one tool for greeting newcomers and some tutors appoint a fellow student to take charge of this.

Some tutors will ask students to close down email and other applications (including games) on their computer, so that they can give their undivided attention to the session. On the other hand, you might wish your students to practise 'cut and paste' from a file during the session or to use the browser to visit particular websites, in which case they will need to keep certain applications open.

Remember there is no body language in distance tutorial work. You might not be as aware of the times when students understand immediately what you are trying to explain, or indeed of the times when they are bored. That means you will certainly need to expend extra effort to ensure that you elicit feedback. You might ask students to show that they are able to follow any discussion either by saying 'Yes', typing 'Y' or by using voting or feedback buttons regularly. Gauge interest in your proposed topic with a poll.

Remember to involve the quieter members of the group. It is easy to overlook quiet students when you cannot see them. Keep a note of who has contributed, so that you can encourage those who have not. Some tutors like to record the names of participants when they first join the session, and then they put a mark against the name of each person who contributes. Refer to participants by name – it helps to keep people awake and involved.

Use turn-taking to pace the discussion and maintain some order. Synchronous sessions for groups generally work better in this way. This has the effect of slowing down the discussion and making proceedings more formal, but it also helps to ensure that there is order rather than chaos. Students ask permission before contributing, either by using a polling button or typing '!' (for a comment). For larger groups you might need a fellow tutor to act as gatekeeper.

At the end

Summarise the session at the end, and give students the encouragement to carry on – motivation is one of the most important reasons for providing synchronous support with students who are studying independently. If the software allows, save the session and circulate the transcript, so that students can refer to it later. Email your students for some feedback and ask if there are any outstanding queries – that can be useful for planning subsequent sessions.

Finally, plan some relaxation for yourself after the session – you'll need it.

TECHNIQUES FOR PARTICULAR TOOLS

Text chat

Chat can be very effective when used in conjunction with other tools. For example, when used with audio, chat can be reserved for comment to individual students or asides on technical problems. It is also effective for short informal sessions or short queries with individual students. However with a group, text chat can be anarchic and unhelpful as an educational tool. Do not have high expectations of content-related learning outcomes for text-only sessions. Consider using asynchronous conferencing for a limited time period for more extended reflective discussion.

Before the session, prepare commonly used phrases, welcome messages or links to additional resources, so that they can be easily pasted into the chat window. Write in short sections, and break up long statements with three dots, to show that there is more to come. To instigate turn-taking, ask students to use '!', and you use 'GA' (Go Ahead) to give them permission to contribute (see box).

CHAT PROTOCOLS

James (moderator): When you have a comment to make, you type !
James: When you have a query, you type ?
James: Break up your comments into small chunks...
James: and put an ellipsis (three dots) to show there is more to come.
Frances: !
Tommy: !
Jane: ?
James: GA Frances, then Tommy, then Jane.
Frances: well I can't help feeling this is all going to take a long time...
Frances: and this is supposed to be synchronous...
Frances: but it feels like, well, asynchronous.
Tommy: I nevre leantto typpe fast.
James: Never mind, doesn't matter, we're glad you made it.

Audio (by telephone or Internet audio)

If you are using audio on its own, you need to ensure that students have been given any necessary diagrams or other visual aids beforehand. Remember that explanations referring to handouts or other resources need to be simple, so that students can follow your verbal instructions.

Equip yourself with a microphone or headset, so that your hands are free to make notes or shuffle papers. Check audio levels before the session if the software allows you to do so.

During the session, don't forget to vary your tone and smile as you speak – just as you would to someone in the room. Such nuances are conveyed with audio. Be aware that silences can be misinterpreted, and you may need to be overt about your intentions; for example, say, 'I'll need to think about that for a moment' rather than simply being silent. You may also need to give your students permission to reflect for a moment or two before responding.

Whiteboard

Prepare visual aids beforehand. Remember how you feel when confronted with bullet lists in a conventional presentation: they will be even more uninteresting at a distance. Make use of graphics, icons, colour – anything to liven up your visual aids. Use the whiteboard for a welcome message to start, together with advice on what to do if the system fails and who to ring. Consider using a whiteboard as you speak, so that you can develop a concept as students watch.

Design activities that concentrate on your visual aids or encourage students to construct their own. Warn students not to edit your visual aids, unless you invite them to: graffiti can be wearisome.

Break-out rooms

Break-out rooms can be useful for small group work and conversations with individual students. When used in conjunction with a plenary space, they allow the tutor to combine group work and report back, just as they might in a face-to-face tutorial.

Prepare rooms in advance of the session and make sure any visual aids are available. Split larger groups into break-out groups of six as soon as possible from the start of the session. Pair up articulate students with those who are less confident. Make sure students understand the activity and the time they have to complete it before they leave for break-out rooms.

RESOURCES

Gaskell, A., George, J., Holland, L., Jordan, S., Simpson, O. and Spirit, J. (2003) *Supporting Students by Telephone*. Open Teaching Toolkit No. 20, Open University (UK).

Macdonald, J., Warnecke, S., Barclay, F., Kilgore, J., Buckland, C. and McLeod, G. (2004) Comparing synchronous tuition in languages and maths/computing. A role for Lyceum. http://kn.open.ac.uk/document. cfm?documentid=5692 (accessed 2 June 2005).

PART III

DEVELOPING INDEPENDENT LEARNERS

CHAPTER 10

THE EXPERIENCE OF BLENDED LEARNING

A blended course may impose a variety of new challenges for students. It is important to have an understanding of what these challenges are so that students can be supported appropriately. In Chapter 4, I described the diversity of courses which use blended learning. I will summarise what we learnt about the students from that survey:

- they are often mature learners;
- they are studying off-campus, either for restricted periods, or all the time;
- during that time they need to work independently;
- they need access to a networked computer, whether off-campus or on-campus; and
- they may need to attend the campus at certain points.

No doubt the most significant change for learners is that they will be expected to study online for part of their course: this often requires more independence and self-direction than they may be used to. The aim of this chapter is to discuss first the practicalities of blended study and then the ways in which students develop as self-directed, independent learners, illustrating this with examples from the blended learning survey and the experiences of students at the Open University (UK) from data I collected as part of my doctorate.

WHAT ARE THE PRACTICAL IMPLICATIONS?

There are various practical implications for students who study a blended course, particularly if they are not on campus and are faced with a new approach to teaching and learning. Such practicalities will not be relevant to all blended courses, but will depend on the environment in which blended learning is introduced and the situation of the student. If your students can reach the campus at all times, you might not find this section relevant.

For example, a study of student perspectives at Wollongong University in Australia, where courses cater simultaneously for on- and off-campus students, revealed a variety of concerns with respect to the following four areas (Lefoe et al., 2002):

- pedagogical
- technical
- student support
- administrative.

Their students recognised that the style of learning differed from conventional university education, with different roles for students and tutors, and they therefore valued clear advice on expectations in this area. While some students lived within a reasonable distance of campus or learning centre, others worked exclusively from home. In this context, they appreciated contact with fellow students, and therefore valued any contribution to the building of a learning community. Those not within easy reach of the campus had problems with access to resources, such as the library, or advice on career planning, which were previously available only to campus-based students. Finally, there were administrative issues, such as being able to enrol at a distance, keeping up-to-date with timetable changes or planning next steps in a path of study, all of which had to be achieved without a visit to the campus.

In addition to these issues, the use of a networked computer for a blended course might require access to equipment from home, at lunchtimes from work or in the evening at the campus. There are implications for the specification of machine they might be using: the sharing of equipment, or study space with family members; the information they might be able to access; their requirement to print out material; the level of frustration due to slow connection speeds; the consequences of firewalls on the accessibility of synchronous tools; or perhaps their need to get technical help at odd times of the day or night.

I thought you might be interested in some tales from part-time students (see box opposite) who adopted a variety of coping strategies in order to accommodate the use of a computer as a part of their study routines. I undertook the original work in 1996, and I therefore decided to circulate my colleagues at the Open University in Scotland in 2005 in order to check the applicability of these tales to current students. The upshot is that many of the challenges faced by students in 1996 are still present for some students on some courses, while other students are fortunate in being able to make use of all the advantages and flexibility that modern technology can offer. I suppose the lesson to learn is that one needs to plan for diversity.

USING A COMPUTER FOR STUDY OFF-CAMPUS

1. Male, working offshore on an oil rig, studied partly in his cabin on the rig and partly at home. He had access to a computer in both places, and found a CD-ROM was very useful because it fitted well into his weight limit on the helicopter transfer to the rig.

2. Female, working part-time and looking after a young family. She studied at home during the day, when she was not at work, and the children were at school, but her computer was rather old and would not run some of the course software.

3. Male, married, one small child, studying in the evenings only. The computer was set up in the hall, as being the only available space in the house near a phone point; so he could only study after nine o'clock in the evening. The computer was bought from a warehouse, and had to be returned three times because of hardware failure; the warehouse offered no helpdesk support.

4. Female, married, in a full-time job with commercial training unit. She did some computer-based study at work, but was somewhat restricted because she was not permitted to run university software on an office workstation. She worked in the dining room at home, in evenings and weekends, sharing a computer with her husband, who was also studying.

5. Social science graduate, doing the course because of changing demands at work; she studied at home, when she needed to stake out time on the computer, which was shared with two teenage children.

6. Unemployed male, horrified at the costs involved in the course, he virtually stopped all conferencing and Internet use after the first telephone bill. Hardware breakdowns meant he was without a computer for three weeks.

7. Computer programmer, female with four dependent children. She studied in lunchtimes at work and at odd periods during the day, for example when waiting for a train or alternatively late in the evening. She preferred to study at home when lying on her bed or in the bath, where obviously a paper copy was needed. Very short of time, no time for reflection, no time for frills, she just wanted that degree.

8. A part-time farmer, female, married with three young children, living on a small island. Any online working tied up the phone line for other members of the family and downloading even small files took an expensive age.

Macdonald (1999)

WHAT MAKES A COMPETENT ONLINE LEARNER?

Arguably the most demanding part of blended learning is the requirement to study online. In this section I explain why this is so and discuss how a blend of support can be used to help students in their learning development.

One of the sometimes unintended consequences of using online media is the choice it offers. Students are exposed to the rich and extensive resources of the web and to the opinions of fellow students and experts in the field. This freedom and choice are available to students at all stages of study at the press of a button, where previously such freedom might only have been offered in final-year project work.

While this could encourage students to study in a more self-directed way than they have previously been used to, it does not necessarily lead to reflective learning if students are not equipped to cope. They need to develop as *e-investigators*.

> On the whole, there is some justification for the belief that new technologies have changed self-directed learning and self-directed learners. On the one hand, they have greatly facilitated access both to rich information resources and to online expertise, and have made it easier for the dedicated, knowledgeable and inquisitive learner to find an extraordinary richness of learning resources. On the other hand, they may lead those who are so inclined to accept partially biased or incompletely understood information, to engage either too deeply or too shallowly with their inquiry, and to rely too heavily on the technology to assist them in knowing what to think and what to believe. (Candy, 2004, pp. 55–56)

Approaches to writing will also be different for students who study online. Online conferencing and email rely on text for communicating, and so it becomes more important than ever before that students learn how to write appropriately. Furthermore, not only can their written work be altered readily, it can also be shared with staff and fellow students. They need to learn to what extent this is appropriate to your course, and also how much to rely on the opinions of fellow students. Students need to be effective *e-writers*.

> One aspect of conferencing which I find useful [...] is the exchange of actual pieces of work. With modern technology it is simple to attach a file of work to a conference message for people to look at and comment on [...] It has proved very interesting and useful to be able to look at how other people have approached activities. (OU student)

Finally, studying online often involves collaborative working. Students need to be able to work together with peers who they do not meet regularly, as well as being able to write appropriately and be discerning in their use of resources. They need to develop as *e-collaborators.*

> *I felt really focused, we had a sense of responsibility and were mutually supportive, I was surprised at the level of feeling. Because we were 'chatting' to each other and balancing each others' arguments ... you had to change your opinion a bit.* (OU student)

The fact is that learning online is not simply about learning how to use a particular tool, such as email or word processing or the virtual learning environment (VLE), although that is often the first step. It involves e-investigating, e-writing and e-collaborating, which are all facets of self-directed learning. In other words, successful blended learners will need to develop as self-directed, reflective learners. You will find a range of activities for giving students practice in e-investigating, e-writing and collaborating in Chapters 12 to 14.

We asked the respondents to our blended learning survey to indicate their students' abilities at the start of the course with respect to basic IT skills and also higher-level skills associated with online study, such as information handling, online discussion and independent study. While most were optimistic about their students' basic IT skills, they were less optimistic about students' competence in online study, and few of their students had previous experience of computer conferencing. The respondents recognised the importance of independent study for the course, although often this was unfamiliar to students. The case studies referred to the influence of their students' previous experiences and more familiar learning cultures.

> *Scaffolding used to gradually move from a F2F, instructor-led ... behaviourist approach to course delivery (initial classroom one day activity) to a more constructivist activity-based learner-centred approach.* (31, Foras Asieanna Saothair, Ireland)

> *... seeking to establish independent learners ... students decide what they want to read, research and learn, and how ... students are part of the development process – therefore they suggest course developments and ideas for coming year ...* (16, Liverpool Hope Univ., UK)

> *Most of them had achieved their bachelor degree from studies in Norway. Here we use problem-based learning as a pedagogical approach. Therefore most of my students are familiar with both group work and independent learning activities. We tell them that 'you are responsible for your own learning, and you are also responsible for your peer students' learning.'* (1, Bergen Univ. College, Norway)

Difficult, during the first semester, because students are not used to studying independently, as they mainly have passed higher schools with a standard school system. And after some years of work experience are not used to study great amounts of new content. (43, Vienna Univ. of Economics and Business Administration, Austria)

While some are very comfortable with this, learning independence is a major deficiency for many. It is an explicit goal of this course to encourage and support this, and students are encouraged to reflect on the importance of appropriate help-seeking and considered learning strategies... Some students take to independent learning, preferring it and making excellent use of the flexibility and individualisation that it offers. Others make decisions to study independently for the wrong reason (e.g., to get out of attending) and can find that they do not manage their learning well. (32, Southern Cross Univ., Australia)

Many of the students have previously experienced only educational opportunities that have been traditional 'chalk and talk', with formal exams of regurgitated information. These may be the older UK students and those who have been educated in other countries and are now recruited to work in UK hospitals. (24, City Univ., UK)

Most felt they were independent learners; in reality, most needed encouragement. (42, Aston Univ., UK)

In fact, encouraging students to develop independence and self-direction in learning is an objective that may involve a lengthy and gradual process under traditional university models of teaching and learning. I will illustrate this point using a classic study which was carried out by Perry (1970) on the development of critical thinking in American college students. He interviewed students at various stages during their college career and coded their comments according to a developmental scheme which described nine 'positions' or models of attitude, starting with what he calls *dualism*, where students saw the world in unqualified 'right/wrong' terms, to *relativism*, where students were able to appreciate diversity in points of view. The gradual development of relativism took a number of years: it did not happen overnight, nor indeed during a single course.

Morgan and Beaty (1997) described a similar gradual process in learning development among Open University (UK) part-time students. They charted the progress of students from when they started to study until graduation, six years later. The students developed gradually over that time in terms of confidence, competence and control over their learning. So, as freshers they were essentially controlled by the institution, with enough confidence to enrol, but not much beyond that. Over the next few years they gradually gained the confidence to question what they were told, and to see how the various parts of content fitted within the whole. By the time they graduated, they had assumed control over their learning, both in terms of what they wanted to learn and the way in which they wanted to learn. They were confident enough to go it alone and competent enough to use the skills and knowledge acquired in new contexts.

My point is that the introduction of online use in courses has tended to accelerate the timescale of learning development for students. The traditional achievement of graduate status reflects the kind of learner which a blended course might seek to develop, and raises the question of how to help students at early stages of their undergraduate career so that they will be able to cope with the demands of more independent study. It is therefore important that we recognise the need to help our students to develop confidence as independent learners as they progress in their studies. It has to form a part of course learning objectives, and is integral to 'learning how to learn'.

There is some evidence that lifelong learners may have an advantage over younger students and Hartley (1998) suggests that they may be better equipped to study independently than younger students. His overview of the research on the performance of mature and younger students indicated that in terms of ability and attitudes to teaching, mature students were broadly similar to younger students but they cheated less. Mature students were more likely to be deep learners and were better at time management than their younger counterparts. On the other hand, if students have been away from formal study for some time they may appreciate some induction into the expectations of independent study and time management, if study routines have to slot in with a working life.

All this has implications for the degrees of freedom or supervision which students are offered, and this can be accommodated by scaling the tasks, so that students learn to develop independence in easy stages. It could also be helpful to adjust the blend of face-to-face and online asynchronous support. Those students who need more supervision or pacing in their studies may benefit from more face-to-face or online synchronous contact. For example, see the comment below from Italy, on a course which caters for 18-year-olds:

> *... face-to-face classes helped to maintain and reinforce the enthusiasm generated online ... in reality, younger students need to be supported and sense a degree of observation and control to maintain momentum to ensure that they learn in a structured and coherent manner.* (3, Istituto Tecnico Agrario Statale, Italy) (www.sol.celeno.it/raga.htm, accessed 20 April 2005)

DOES ONLINE LEARNING SUIT ALL STUDENTS?

The story does not end there, because a variety of other factors may influence the approach which students adopt in their studies. These factors might be related to their previous experiences, the reasons why they are studying, their reaction to the university or college environment or to fellow students. In fact, Taylor et al. (1981) coined the term 'orientation to study' to describe the variety of motivations behind student approaches. They argued that students may demonstrate a combination of several orientations to study and that these can vary throughout their student careers. I wonder if you recognise any of your own students in Table 10.1? Have a look at the list of aims and concerns. Such factors must surely influence the success or otherwise of any teaching strategy which you might devise for them. Some students may be more likely than others to relish choice in their study, and therefore to engage more readily with independent study at certain points in their career.

Table 10.1   Orientations to study (Taylor et al., 1981, p. 4. Reproduced with kind permission from the Open University, UK)

Orientation	Interest	Aim	Concerns
Vocational	Intrinsic	Training	Relevance of course to career
	Extrinsic	Qualification	Recognition of worth of qualification
Academic	Intrinsic	Follow intellectual interest	Room to choose work, stimulating lectures
Personal	Intrinsic	Self improvement	Challenge, interesting material
	Extrinsic	Proof of capability	Feedback, passing the course
Social	Intrinsic	Have a good time	Facilities for sport and social activities

There may also be cultural influences on the acceptability of self-directed study. For example, Zhang and Perris (2004) describe student perceptions of online courses in 11 open universities in Asia. While students were positive about the flexibility and accessibility offered by the courses, and liked to be able to share resources and ideas with each other, many of them were uncomfortable with self-directed learning because they were more used to didactic instruction.

The practical implications of all this are that not all students at all levels will necessarily appreciate the demands of independent online study, and it may be that you need to consider ways of ensuring that students are aware of the implications before they sign up for your course. To accommodate less confident students, activities could be scaled down so that they are less demanding and afford less flexibility. You could also ensure that your blend includes sufficient face-to-face or online synchronous contact to support the needs of the more apprehensive students.

To illustrate these points, I have included two sketches of Open University (UK) students who were required to study in an open resource-based approach on a second level course. Many students found the course demanding and you will see that one student coped rather better than the other because he had plenty of experience of independent study and was highly strategic in his approach to choice within the course. The other student was simply lost in a sea of possibilities.

STUDENT REACTIONS TO INDEPENDENT ONLINE STUDY

Michael

Michael was in his sixth year of part-time study, having followed Maths and Computing courses, and was hoping for a first-class degree. He had a young family and worked in London, so found that study time was at a premium.

New skills which he felt had been acquired on the course included researching; using other authors' material and producing a reasoned argument. He had used the Internet previously, but only in a limited way for recreation, and as a result of this course found it a valuable source of information. He was less enthusiastic about the CD-ROM library and had found the articles difficult to trace. Not surprisingly he had no difficulty with technical skills associated with operating hardware and software, but found that he needed to adapt his study time to the need to read in front of a monitor; this meant that he had to work more weekends, instead of using odd times during the day. He felt that the course was significantly more time-consuming than previous 60-point courses.

The assignments had helped him to focus on the important issues:

I used to make conscientious notes, but as I moved jobs, I made less and less notes because of time pressures. During the course, as I'm studying I think 'here is something I want to learn and need to understand'. If there is any tuning, it's for assignments, I mark sections as I go along which might be of relevance to the next assignment.

This student was clearly very able and had already completed a number of courses which gave him a good background in the technology. The resource-based approach presented new challenges in terms of researching material, and a new approach to writing, but the impression was that he was well equipped to meet these challenges and made good use of the assignments as a way of practising these skills and focusing his reading.

Jane

Jane was planning to return to work, since her children had started school, and was following a degree course in order to train as a teacher. She had studied the social science Level One course in the previous year, and planned to take two 60-point courses next year, in the hope that she could work towards a degree in four years.

She had had no previous experience with electronic searching and this was one of her reasons for picking the course. As for study methods, she found that even by the end of the course she preferred to print off material, and had not become used to screen-based reading. When interviewed at the start of the course, she did not feel she was particularly good at skim reading and found the resource-based approach very time-consuming:

> I have to read everything thoroughly so it takes an awfully long time! I like to satisfy myself that I know it thoroughly.

By the end of the course she was more confident about picking out relevant or important information, and believed that the information-handling assignment had been helpful in teaching her ways of looking for significant words and phrases when reading. She was also confident in her ability to use conferencing for collaborative learning, although unenthusiastic about its use of a medium of communication with other students.

In spite of the guidance given to students she continued to find the resource-based approach very time-consuming, because of its open endedness. Her previous course, which had been considerably more directed in terms of content, had been a poor preparation: 'It almost did me a disservice'. She found herself floundering with resource-based learning. Clearly this student, although very determined to succeed, was ill-prepared for this approach to study, and might have benefited more had it been introduced at a later stage in her academic career.

Macdonald (1999)

Having described the student perspective and the development of self-directed learning in this chapter, I go on in Chapter 11 to outline ways in which appropriate course design can support students as blended learners.

IN SUMMARY

I have made the following points about the learner's experience of blended learning:

- A variety of practical considerations are faced by students who undertake blended learning and may not be situated on the campus at all times.

These can include access to pedagogical, technical or administrative support which was previously designed for campus-based students.

- The use of computers, and particularly of online study, presents challenges for students, particularly where they are not using equipment within the institution, underlining the need for flexibility in course design and a sympathetic approach to tutor-mediated support.
- Learning online requires students to study more independently than they may previously have been used to – successful blended learners will be self-directed, reflective learners.
- Online learning may not suit all students, and familiarity with independent study can assist chances of success.
- I have concentrated here on the concerns of the lifelong learner, as a reflection of those who contributed to the blended learning survey. However, blended learning offers the opportunity to tailor the course to the needs of other students. A blended course might cater to less experienced students by adjusting the balance of asynchronous to synchronous support.

RESOURCES

Candy, P. (2004) Linking thinking – Self-directed learning in the Digital Age. http://www.dest.gov.au/research/publications/linking_thinking/exec_summary.htm (accessed 23 May 2005).

Hartley, J. (1998) *Learning and Studying. A Research Perspective* (London, Routledge).

Lefoe, G., Gunn, C., and Hedberg, J. (2002) Recommendations for teaching in a distributed learning environment: The students' perspective. *Australian Journal of Educational Technology* **18** (1), pp. 40–56.

Macdonald, J. (1999) *Appropriate assessment for resource based learning in networked environments* (unpublished PhD thesis, Open University, UK).

Morgan, A. and Beaty, L. (1997) The world of the learner. In *The Experience of Learning*, ed. Marton, F., Hounsell, D. and Entwistle, N. (Edinburgh, Scottish Academic Press, second edition).

Perry, W.G. (1970) *Forms of Intellectual and Ethical Development in the College Years* (New York, Holt Rhinehart & Winston).

Taylor, E., Morgan, A.R. and Gibbs, G. (1981) The orientations of Open University students to their studies. *Teaching at a Distance* **20**, pp. 3–12.

Zhang, W. and Perris, K. (2004) Researching the efficacy of online learning: a collaborative effort amongst scholars in Asian open universities. *Open Learning* **19** (3), pp. 247–264.

CHAPTER 11

COURSE DESIGN FOR BLENDED LEARNING

In Chapter 10 I described some of the challenges which might face students who are confronted with self-directed study within a blended course. The aim of this chapter is to discuss strategies to keep students 'on course' and ways of helping them to develop as competent blended learners. I draw on the literature in this field and have illustrated it with the experiences of contributors to the blended learning survey. This chapter serves as an introduction to the following three chapters, which contain a range of practical ideas and activities for learning development when using online media.

KEEPING STUDENTS ON COURSE AND IN TUNE

You might expect that students faced with a climate of freedom and choice will be likely to 'vote with their feet', choosing those aspects of your course which they consider best suit their needs, and leaving other parts which they may perceive as less relevant. This could have implications for their attendance or participation in either online or classroom activity. The extent to which you are prepared to countenance this will depend on the objectives of the course and what you hope your students will achieve. But having offered them choice and variety in their study, it will be important to help them to choose appropriately.

A blended course may encourage students to learn in new and unfamiliar ways, using a variety of tools and techniques. However, students need to understand what it is they are expected to learn, how they are expected to get there and in what timescale. This is particularly important if they are to be faced with a new regime which offers them greater flexibility, a more self-directed approach or perhaps less synchronous contact time with staff than they have previously been used to.

Those who contributed to the blended learning survey were clear that appropriate induction was one of the most important factors contributing to the success of their strategy because the approach was likely to be unfamiliar to students. Not only did students need to be competent in using the online tools, but they also needed guidance on boundaries, expectations and the level of commitment required. They also needed to understand where and when they would be expected to study, the degree of independence and self-direction required, and the extent to which they would work with their peers online.

There is a variety of ways in which these aims might be met. This is not an exhaustive list, and these ideas are certainly not new, but they acquire new importance in this context, in helping students to understand what is required of them in an unfamiliar learning environment.

Student induction and pre-course information

Course descriptions need to be clear about objectives, the expectations on students for independent or collaborative study and attendance or participation, whether online or in class. Some courses do this in face-to-face induction sessions, where students may be introduced to the online tools as well as to each other. Others organise diagnostic tests or offer pre-course counselling. The following extracts illustrate a range of strategies:

- *Pre-module questionnaire distributed to discover the following information about the participants:*
  - *Virtual learning environment: their access to the Internet, preferred time of access*
  - *Basic IT skills: word processing, email, etc.*
  - *Internet skills: navigating web browsers, using search engines, etc.*
  - *Prior knowledge/experience about the area of designing online learning, participating in asynchronous or synchronous discussions*
  - *Preferred method of working: individually/independently, small group work-*
  - *Motivation for doing the module.*

(18, Dublin Inst. of Technology, Ireland)

... providing pre-course information so that participants were clear about what they could expect to get out of the course. An online booking form was used to collect relevant information. I also speak to potential participants to ascertain their requirements and level of commitment. It is essential that participants understand what their commitment is ... (11, Univ. Manchester, UK)

We actually run some orientation sessions to teach students how to participate in online discussion ... we model Salmon's model, and ask students to analyse their posting's content. I have just completed an online version for orientation for students to using online discussion forums, which aims to quickly move them to stage 3 of Salmon's model. There is also a section for instructors. (48, Univ. Sydney, Australia)

... clearly defining the roles and responsibilities of a student in a student-centred as opposed to a teacher-centred class. ... For the second group that began the programme I took the time to clearly lay out these responsibilities and the transition was much smoother and quicker. (37, Hainan Radio and TV Univ., PR China)

Course study guides

Students benefit from a clear structure and schedule, so that they are able to see what they need to do and when. Some courses will also offer a commentary on the various activities and resources, in this way providing a pathway through the course and a link with learning outcomes. The example in Table 11.1 shows a study schedule which was designed to encourage students to plan their time appropriately between lectures, tutorials and self-study from CD or website. In order to monitor progress against this schedule, students are periodically asked to complete anonymous confidence logs. Students rate their confidence against the learning objectives, in order to allow staff to identify areas of collective difficulty.

Learning contracts

Learning contracts (see Figure 11.1) encourage students to take responsibility for their learning and reflect on their own objectives and responsibilities with respect to the course. They develop a strategy for meeting the course learning objectives and address practical challenges: for example, how and when they will study.

Table 11.1   An example of a study schedule (Reproduced with kind permission by Dr Peter Ball, Design, Manufacture and Engineering Management. © University of Strathclyde, 2005)

		Strathclyde University (UK) Manufacturing Operations Management			
Week	Day	Activity	Study topic/activity	CD	Est. hours*
1	Tuesday	Lecture	Introduction to the class and study mode		1
	Friday	Self study	Shop floor layout (revision)	Production	1
2	Tuesday	Lecture	Material overview and progress check		1
	Friday	Self study	Capacity management	Production	1
			Production scheduling	Production	
3	Tuesday	Tutorial	Scheduling		1
	Friday	Self study	Organising production	Production	1.5
			Push systems	Production	
			Pull systems	Production	
			Push and pull compared	Production	
4	Tuesday	Workshop	Kanban demonstration		1
	Friday	Self study	Batch size	Production	1.5
			Set up time reduction	Production	
			Just In Time	Production	
			Conclusion	Production	
5	Tuesday	Lecture	Planning overview inc. MRP, MRPII, ERP		1
	Friday	Self study	Planning	Materials	3
			MRP model	Materials	
6	Tuesday	Tutorial	MRP		1
	Friday	Self study	Support functions (inventory)	Materials	1.5
7	Tuesday	Tutorial	Inventory		1
	Friday	Self study	Support functions (capacity planning)	Materials	1
			Conclusion	Materials	
8	Tuesday	Tutorial	Capacity planning		1
	Friday	Self study	Demand management	Customer needs	1
9	Tuesday	Lecture	MPS and forecasting overview		1
	Friday	Self study	Forecasting	Customer needs	1.5
10	Tuesday	Tutorial	Forecasting		1
	Friday	Self study	Master planning	Customer needs	2
			Conclusions	Customer needs	
11	Tuesday	Tutorial	MPS		1
	Friday	Self study	Optimised production technology	Web-based	2
			Period batch control	Web-based	
12	Tuesday	Tutorial	OPT and PBC		1
	Friday	Lecture	Revision/exam papers		1

*Estimated hours indicates the attendance/study time to progress through the study materials *once*. It is expected that students will spend a total of 100 hours on attendance, self-study, tutorial questions, revision and exam prep. There are two assignments prior to the exam ... The inventory and production planning assignment [international team project] takes place in weeks 6–11 in teams of 4 students – 2 from Iowa State and 2 from Strathclyde, supported by the Strathclyde LauLima Environment and the Iowa State Engineering Learning Portal.

Suffolk College, UK. Foundation Degree by Employment Based Independent Study

Learning Agreement Level 1

Student: ....

Employer: ....

Specialist tutor: ....

Subject area: ....

Summary of prior learning and/or experience
(Here students should discuss factors leading up to the proposed study; for example, what experience they have in the methods they have chosen and the subject area they will be investigating, evidence that they are capable of carrying out the research/activities)

Justification for proposed programme of study
(Students should justify their choice in terms of the amount of subject material and other resources available and its currency, and should indicate its relevance to their employers and their own developmental/personal needs)

Description of the proposed study, including taught modules, negotiated studies, specialist subjects and research activities.
(This is where the student sets out their intentions for the submission, what they will be investigating and producing; for example, an essay of 3,500 words that discusses theories of motivation and how they relate to a small manufacturing business. It also includes statements of the student's solution to the problem, 'How am I going to produce evidence that I can meet the planned activities?')

Learning and assessment outcomes with assessment schedule
(Informed by generic outcomes for each module, which can be found in student handbooks, these need to be contextualised for each module planned. The student will need to agree assessment deadlines in line with Assessment Board requirements.)

An exploration of the resource implications and indicative reading list
(Here we would expect the student to discuss resources in terms of, for example, time, finance, access; discuss all issues such as costs involved in inter-library loans, photocopying, travel costs, etc. Access issues include a consideration of ethics, confidentiality, whose permission they have sought regarding access etc. This is where the student can request input from the tutor, such as looking over a draft, or providing copies of some material not in the library, or an introduction to an interviewee. This section is also the place to clarify complicating issues, such as collaborative work in a small group)

Submission date: ....

Second marker: ....

Figure 11.1   Example learning contract (Reproduced with kind permission of Peter Funnell, Suffolk College, UK)

Aligning course objectives with activities and assessment

By ensuring that the course objectives are aligned with activities, whether online or face-to-face, and particularly with the assessment, students are clear where the course priorities lie. Many case studies reflected this concern.

> *The activity is an integral part of the course (not an add-on). Participation is not graded, however those who do not participate are disadvantaged. There are complementary needs (the need to be exposed to more literature and the need to try out one's own understanding of a paper). Collaboration rather than competition.* (7, Univ. Canterbury, New Zealand)

> *Making the online activities an integral part of the module i.e. writing them into the paper pack and not giving a written answer was crucial ... A consideration for development of future modules is whether online contribution should be assessed to encourage participation.* (30, Univ. Dundee, UK)

> *... emphasise the importance of each activity with respect to their learning outcomes – make the use of a VLE compulsory – structure tasks and communication tools/techniques to correspond with each other* (9, Middlesex Univ., UK)

> *Critical to success is clear linkage to assessment. If credit for time online cannot be gained then participants will not do it.* (6, Oxford Brookes Univ., UK)

CONSTRUCTIVE ALIGNMENT AND LEARNING DESIGN

This last concern is well founded, and needs further explanation. Biggs' (2003) influential model of constructive alignment is based on two ideas: constructivism and alignment. The theory of constructivism maintains that students learn by constructing their own understanding through learning activities. In other words, students themselves have to be active in developing their own understanding. The way in which they do this is related to a variety of factors, including their individual context, by which I mean the experiences they have had in the past, their motivation and the purposes to which they intend to put the new knowledge.

An effective way of getting students to engage in learning is to devise activities in which they have to take an active part. Students are more likely to learn effectively when they are presented with situations in which they construct meaning for themselves and relate any new information to the experiences they already have. While the more academic students in any group will do this anyway, the rest need encouragement and support. With increasing diversity in university or college intake, this becomes more important than it has ever been in the past. So rather than 'opening their heads, and pouring in the content' and then testing students to see how much remains at the end of the course, many course writers are turning their hands to activities in which students can 'learn by doing'. It is far more effective than giving out facts for them to memorise and reproduce in an assignment. It places emphasis on the development of skills which students will need in the workplace and helps them develop as lifelong learners.

Biggs suggests that the most effective approach to course design is when the teaching method, assessment and learning activities are aligned to learning objectives. This means that students are what he calls 'trapped in a web of consistency'.

> *In aligned teaching there is maximum consistency throughout the system. The curriculum is stated in the form of clear objectives, which state the level of understanding required, rather than simply a list of topics to be covered. The teaching methods are chosen that are likely to realise those objectives; you get students to do the things that the objectives nominate. Finally, the assessment tasks address the objectives, so that you can test to see if the students have learned what the objectives state they should be learning.* (Biggs, 2003, p. 27)

Such a principle would hold true regardless of the environment you chose to work in, whether in a classroom or in an online medium. However, it has acquired a new relevance because it underpins the current interest in learning design, which as a concept is gaining credibility in e-learning circles. According to Britain, learning design means:

> *... new possibilities for increasing the quality and variety of teaching and learning within an e-learning context:*
>
> - *The first general idea behind learning design is that people learn better when actively involved in doing something (i.e. are engaged in a learning activity).*
> - *The second idea is that learning activities may be sequenced or otherwise structured carefully and deliberately in a learning workflow to promote more effective learning.*
> - *The third idea is that it would be useful to be able to record 'learning designs' for sharing and reuse in the future.* (Britain, 2004, p. 2)

Associated with these ideas is the development of standards to provide a platform-independent model for tasks and activities, and the sequence in which they are undertaken. In this way, both the tasks and the sequence in which they are carried out can be stored and reused in a variety of situations. I believe the concept of learning design has particular relevance to blended learning, because it lays emphasis on the relationship between activities and the need for coherence between different course elements.

To reiterate, the upshot of both constructive alignment and learning design is that in a successful blended strategy all elements of the course, including the assessment, are consciously designed to reflect learning objectives. This is achievable through a pathway of related activities that help students to develop their skills and understanding in simple steps. Such activities might take place in a classroom, or where appropriate might take the form of lab sessions, presentations by students or a discussion of coursework. In an online environment, tutor-mediated activities can be supplemented by activities that use online tools such as formative assessment packages or simulations.

THE ROLES OF ASSESSMENT

In Chapters 6 and 8, I referred to assessment-framed activity as an important model of tutor-mediated support for both asynchronous and synchronous online environments. Somehow, it seems much more difficult to make learning activities successful in an online environment than it is in a classroom. Of course, in the classroom you can always shut the door, so that your students are less likely to escape before the end of the session. In an online environment you can never be entirely certain that your students will walk through the door in the first place. And within a blended strategy there are often alternatives for students, who may decide that they prefer tutorial contact by other routes: they didn't, after all, sign up for a completely online experience. While some students will participate enthusiastically without much encouragement, others may give up or never attempt to begin.

The lesson is that if it is important that all (or at least, most) students undertake your online activities, then those activities need to be linked overtly to the development of an assignment. Assignments represent the only time when online learning activities will be undertaken by the majority of students, and are the crucial points at which feedback can be focused. All this underlines the importance of formulating appropriate course objectives, supported by authentic assessment design to support those objectives, and encouraging students not only to develop an understanding of course concepts, but also to develop the discernment to study effectively in a blended environment.

Assessment can and should support student learning in a range of ways. It is emphatically not just about assessing online participation.

It should reflect course philosophy and course learning outcomes

Beyond its acknowledged importance in judging the quality of students' work, assessment has powerful formative potential in helping students learn how to learn effectively. If a course employs a blended teaching strategy, then students will need to develop self-judgment and critical abilities. The assessment can then be deployed to help them develop, unless of course they already possess these attributes in good measure.

It can create learning opportunities at critical points

If a course is designed around learning activities, then it is important that the students undertake those activities in order to engage with the learning process and derive benefit from the course. Students need to be in no doubt that any activities which you regard as critical do indeed form an important part of what they study. The maxim 'assessment drives learning' is as true in this context as it has always been in more traditional education, and the trick is to create learning opportunities that students will find difficult to resist.

Where collaborative work is involved, it is even more important that all students participate, because any inactivity on the part of some students directly impacts on, and is immensely irritating to, fellow students. The close integration of activities with assessment will ensure students' participation at critical points in the course.

It provides a vital opportunity for feedback

By conceptualising learning activities and feedback on them as part of the learning defined by an assignment, you help students to complete the reflective learning cycle. In this context it is important to articulate in course learning outcomes the processes that students are expected to undertake if their development is to be supported during the course. You can provide practice in the development of skills and literacies, and incremental support and feedback over linked assignments. We know that while some students are happy to undertake activities on their own, it is important for many students to have a 'guide on the side' who will provide feedback on their learning and encouragement to continue. Whether in an online or face-to-face environment, feedback on learning may be provided through contact with peers or a tutor, and of course the online environment may offer the option of automated formative assessment packages.

There are many useful lessons in the literature on the design of assessment for developing reflective learning; for example, Nicol and Macfarlane-Dick (2004) summarise seven sensible principles of good feedback practice which can contribute to the development of self-direction and a reflective approach in learners.

SEVEN PRINCIPLES OF GOOD FEEDBACK PRACTICE

Feedback:
1. helps clarify what good performance is;
2. facilitates the development of self assessment in learning;
3. delivers high-quality information to students about their learning;
4. encourages teacher and peer dialogue around learning;
5. encourages positive motivational beliefs and self esteem;
6. provides opportunities to close the gap between current and desired performance;
7. provides information to teachers that can be used to help shape the teaching.

Nicol and Macfarlane-Dick (2004)

They suggest a number of well tested techniques for providing better feedback, many of which are applicable in a networked environment. Very often students do not understand what is required of them and need to see how the requirements of the course or the assignment relate to what they have been able to achieve so far. Such feedback might take place:

- with the group, or to individuals;
- in a classroom, or online;
- in a computer conference, or by email;
- as automated formative assessment;
- as comments on paper-based or emailed assignments.

It might take the form of:

- comments on activities leading to assessment;
- input to a discussion of assignment criteria;
- 'feed forward' on interim assignment drafts from tutor or from peer review;
- general hints to the group on study skills;
- model answers to illustrate good writing;
- assignment feedback to individual students;

- group feedback and input into group discussion of feedback;
- advice for the next assignment.

I will discuss these ideas, as they relate to learning development for blended learners in the next three chapters. I have divided my account into e-investigating, e-writing and e-communicating, but the three are closely related and there is some overlap between the three areas.

IN SUMMARY

In this chapter, I have discussed a variety of strategies for course design which have come into use in order to encourage students to study appropriately in a blended environment. There is really nothing especially new here: these ideas are based on a wealth of knowledge and understanding built up over years of experience in student learning with and without learning technologies. The trick is to apply these lessons to a new context. I made the following points:

- Many of the principles of good course design for self-directed learning will be applicable to blended learning.
- There are various ways in which students can be channelled to study appropriately. I referred to appropriate induction, study guides, learning contracts and the alignment of course objectives with activities and assessment.
- Assessment design has a particularly critical role in reflecting learning outcomes, creating learning opportunities and providing the basis for formative feedback.

RESOURCES

Biggs, J. (2003) *Teaching for Quality Learning at University* (Buckingham, SRHE/OUP, second edition).

Britain, S. (2004) A review of learning design: Concept, specifications and tools. A report for the JISC E-learning Pedagogy Programme http://www.jisc.ac.uk/uploaded_documents/ACF1ABB.doc (accessed 23 May 2005)

Nicol, D.J. and Macfarlane-Dick, D. (2004). Rethinking formative assessment in HE: A theoretical model and seven principles of good feedback practice. http://www.heacademy.ac.uk/assessment/ASS051D_SENLEF_model.doc (accessed 22 May 2005).

CHAPTER 12

DEVELOPING E-INVESTIGATORS

With widespread access to the resources of the Internet it is common practice for students to make use of electronic information resources for their studies. While you may be delighted that they are prepared to widen their horizons in this way, it may also be alarming if they alight on inappropriate material, or lack the ability to select and interpret this material wisely, or perhaps see it as a golden opportunity to download material that they can pass off as their own. The aim of this chapter is to describe what is known about information literacy, to outline the ways in which electronic resources are used for study, and then to suggest how you might help your students to use the resources of the web effectively in a blended strategy.

ADVANTAGES OF ELECTRONIC RESOURCES

The prospect of using resources in electronic form is very appealing to both staff and students. The many benefits include:

- saving queues and pressure on resources at the library;
- availability of resources all the time, including unsocial hours;
- readily updatable;
- hyperlinks which can lead to related information of interest;
- the option to personalise resources, so that students only receive information of relevance to their needs;
- interactivity, for example diagnostic quizzes, to check on progress and achievement;
- multimedia, such as graphics, audio and video, as well as text. This often makes them more interesting; for example, a simulation programme can give the look and feel of some dangerous procedure;
- can take up less space than paper copy and are easier to keep in order;

- can give students practice in identifying what is relevant and useful; and
- a greater choice in study routes, giving students freedom to follow their own interests, building study skills and a more independent approach to study.

HOW DO STUDENTS COME TO BE E-INVESTIGATORS?

Since the resources of the web have become within any networked student's reach, there has been much concern to help students to make effective use of them. In this context, the term 'information literacy' is in use, particularly in the USA and Australia. Snavely and Cooper (1997) refer to it as the involvement of learners in:

- knowing when they have a need for information;
- identifying information needed to address a given problem or issue;
- finding needed information;
- evaluating the information;
- organising the information; and
- using the information effectively to address the problem or issues at hand.

Success in information literacy is influenced by many factors, which are certainly not likely to be achievable in one course, or indeed during one year of study. That relates to the comments I made on learning development in Chapter 10. Candy (2000) refers to these factors under two headings: the context and the individual.

The context

There are different types of information that will be appropriate in different situations, and for answering different types of queries. So the kind of information that is appropriate to answer a well-defined question such as 'What is the circumference of the earth?' will not be the same kind of information that is needed to meet the needs of an extended critique of methods of measuring the circumference of the earth. If you have not given students a list of recommended reading, they may need help in deciding what are appropriate types of information to use as resources for queries in your discipline.

In order to evaluate the relevance and applicability of the information they retrieve, a knowledge of the discipline is critical. The upshot is that a student might be information-literate in, say, computer science, but this will not make them a competent investigator in mediaeval history. If your students do not have much in the way of discipline knowledge, then they will need help in deciding what is likely to be relevant.

At a more advanced level, where students are required to engage in independent project work, there is an expectation that they will be able to recognise the gaps in their knowledge ('knowing when you have a need for information') in order to establish what they need to find out. This recognition, together with an understanding of the framework of the discipline, provides the basis for further exploration and research.

The individual

It is rather a circular argument, but those students who are confident in independent self-directed study will often be those who are most confident as investigators. While this reflects the stage in learning development reached by the student, it is also related to the orientation and motivation of the individual. Some students simply prefer to find things out for themselves, perhaps because they are studying for interest or pleasure. Others do not appreciate the approach because they are studying to get a qualification and have little time for time-consuming elements of the course. That relates to the comments I made on orientation to study in Chapter 10.

Staff and students currently make use of electronic resources in ways that are appropriate at different stages in a student's course of study. McDowell (2002) identifies three common practices which you may find familiar:

- *The electronic academic library*: Some tutors will use web resources as an electronic equivalent of the institution's library, and identify resources they know will be particularly of use to their students. This might take the form of the traditional reading list, or possibly links from a course website. The resources might be academic papers from electronic journals or websites from reliable sources. At any rate, the principle is that the tutor will recommend a variety of resources for enhancing and broadening students' understanding of the course, and this ensures that students are introduced to appropriate resources.

- *Bringing the world into the classroom*: On some courses, students are encouraged to make use of primary information resources such as the letters of a writer, or perhaps official statistics, so that they can undertake authentic tasks. The availability of these resources in electronic form has made such opportunities possible, where previously there were restrictions in access to this material.
- *The unregulated electronic information world*: Students may often of their own accord locate resources on the web for their written assignments. They are also commonly in contact with fellow students, who are themselves a significant source of information, encouragement or advice. The extent to which they are successful in identifying and evaluating appropriate resources in this context can be variable, and they often benefit from help in learning how to develop their critical and interpretive ability.

You can see how the development of e-investigating is closely related to e-communicating and collaborating in the example below.

BONA FIDE RESOURCES? AN EXCHANGE BETWEEN STUDENTS IN A NETWORKED COURSE

From: Shaun O'Donnelly
Subject: Average CO2 emissions per person

I have worked out my average weekly personal CO2 emissions (km travelled in my car, solo, multiplied by CO2 emitted by my car per km). I'd like to know if it's comparatively high or low – does anyone know if there is info held anywhere on average CO2 emissions ??

From: Jasmine Templar
Subject: Re: Average CO2 emissions per person

I do have some (minimal) data about this. In general the CO2/person (from all sources) for 'western' countries is about 3–10 tonnes/yr and transport makes up a very big part of that. I hope that this helps.
Jasmine

From: Sonia Smyth
Subject: Global Warming & Crop Production Lecture

Maybe you would be interested in this event in London?
'Global warming in a chaotic climate – can we be sure?'

Admission free – no ticket or advance booking required.
Sonia

BTW: Thanks to Martin for the matrix... an interesting presentation! :) and thanks to Terry for the US pyramid link.

More radically, the course may require students to study by undertaking activities online, often working collaboratively, and drawing on a collection of resources in electronic form, as a direct substitute for written course materials or lectures. Such resource-based courses offer much potential in a networked environment, with the ready accessibility of a wide diversity of resources on the web, and the scope for new ways to access and combine information and to present information in a variety of different media. They provide students with greater latitude in their use of resources, and a greater degree of independence in the way in which they undertake their studies and present their work.

> *Electronic forms of information are very exciting: there is the potential for unique interpretation and for constructing an individual knowledge base. Electronic storage and retrieval makes it all so much more efficient, and it allows you to be more flexible in your arguments: if one argument doesn't stand up, you can easily search for materials to support another.* (OU student)

These approaches are commonly introduced towards the end of the undergraduate course of study, when it is deemed that students will be able to cope with the open-ended approach. At the same time, there is a good argument for helping students to develop their abilities in this area throughout an undergraduate course of study, particularly since, with the advent of web-based resources, they will make use of these resources whether we invite them to or not.

> *I find the learning process more meaningful if I have played an active role in it. I enjoy the feeling of discovery as I come across new information. It's like a curtain lifting, or a new horizon opening up.* (OU student)

There are two approaches to supporting students to develop as e-investigators. One is to offer generic study skills advice, and the second is to embed the practice of e-investigation within course assessment so that the process is closely related to the course concepts being studied. There is usually room for both strategies.

In terms of generic advice, many institutions have put in place information literacy training for students as generic skills support and there is no doubt that there are useful lessons to be learnt in this way. Topics commonly covered include the use of appropriate search engines or online databases, the types of information available or approaches to evaluating resources. The rest of this chapter describes ways in which learning development for e-investigators can be embedded in activities as part of the course.

DECIDING ON RELEVANCE

To develop a critical approach to resources in your subject, you might use an activity in evaluating a shortlist of 'kitemarked' resources, for which you have checked the currency of the links. This activity could be used in a classroom or by email between pairs of students.

SELECTING AND EVALUATING INFORMATION FROM A READING LIST

In preparation for assignment y, shortlist three resources from the reading list which you think will be of most relevance. For each of these resources, comment on:
- why it is relevant to the assignment;
- the likely credibility of the author, and why;
- the web address (reflecting the nature and quality of information); and
- when the resource was last updated.

Now swap your notes with your buddy and:
- comment on their choices; and
- submit your notes, and mention one idea from your buddy's comments.

Students might find a checklist, such as the PROMPT list opposite, a helpful way of approaching the task of evaluating resources.

SEARCHING FOR INFORMATION

As students become more confident and more advanced in their understanding of the subject, they might be required to undertake their own searching to provide material for an assignment. At this stage, they will appreciate support first in learning an appropriate use of the available tools, and second in devising sensible searching strategies.

DEVELOPING SENSIBLE SEARCH STRATEGIES

Compare the use of two different search engines used to collect material for an essay on a course issue, and comment on the usefulness of four sources you have found.
- For each search engine, list the keywords used, and any changes you made to your search strategy, including the reasons for your changes.
- Select two sites which you regard as useful and relevant to your essay, and two which were less so.
- For each site, comment on why you believe them to be useful, or not, and explain what criteria you have used to judge their value.

Write outline headings for your essay based on the material you have found.

EVALUATING INFORMATION: PROMPT

Presentation
Is the information clearly communicated?
Look at language, layout, structure, etc.

Relevance
Does the information match the needs of the searcher?
Look at the introduction or overview. What is it mainly about?

Objectivity
Is the author's position of interest made clear?
Look for an introduction or overview. Do the writers state their position on the issue? Is the language emotive? Are there hidden, vested interests?

Method (research reports only)
Is it clear how the data was collected?
Were the methods appropriate? Do you trust it?

Provenance
Is it clear where the information has come from?
Can you identify the authors or organisations? How was it published?

Timeliness
Is it clear when the information was produced?
Does the date of the information meet your requirements? Is it obsolete?

(Reproduced from SAFARI (Skills in Accessing, Finding And Reviewing Information; http://www.open.ac.uk/safari) with kind permission from the Open University, UK)

This assignment is based on a design for a second-level undergraduate technology course, in which students were encouraged to use a search engine to select a limited number of academic papers to provide material for an essay on a course issue. Not only were they expected to write the essay, they also had to reflect on the process of selection and describe how they chose the papers. In this way, we wanted to encourage them to develop some critical and analytical skills, as well as skills in using the search engine, alongside a developing knowledge and understanding of the subject field.

Students were expected to undertake activities in which they practised use of the basic search tools. The assignment effectively provided them with an irresistible opportunity to learn.

> *I had used the Internet but have never done anything like this before. I'm getting into it now. If the assignment wasn't there I wouldn't have bothered. It was quite a good idea to put that in.* (OU student)

However, we discovered that it was only when they were required to prepare for the assignment that they started to undertake the searching activities we had recommended. Unfortunately, because many were stumbling with the basic tools they did not do as well as they might have done (Macdonald *et al.*, 2001). The practical implications are that if you are unable to bring students into a classroom in order to ensure that they undertake preliminary exercises, then such exercises need to be written into a series of assignments.

USING RESOURCES APPROPRIATELY

If students are given more freedom than is afforded by a reading list or a list of acceptable links to resources, then they need to learn how to choose resources that are appropriate to the task. They could be encouraged to develop an annotated bibliography (see box) on a course topic, by linking course concepts with other resources. The bibliography gives students an opportunity to practise appropriate referencing and, if constructed online, might include hyperlinks to full text material, or other resources such as conference messages or entries in a reflective log. In this context students may appreciate a guide to appropriate referencing, so that they know what is acceptable practice in your institution.

PREPARING AN ANNOTATED BIBLIOGRAPHY

As preparation for your report on topic i, produce a bibliography of up to 10 resources, which must include three references to course texts, three references to web-based resources and four references to computer conference messages or entries in your reflective log.

For each resource, include:
- the date when you accessed it;
- a note of the author, provenance and date last updated;
- two sentences to describe the content;
- two sentences to justify its relevance;
- a sentence to explain the intended readership;
- a hyperlink to the original document, if there is one.

Write two paragraphs of guidance notes for future students on the effective choice and use of resources in assignments.

About plagiarism

The ease with which material from the Internet can be retrieved, cut and pasted into notes or assignments means that students need a good understanding of what is meant by plagiarism and how to avoid it. Plagiarism is often simply defined as passing off someone else's work as your own. Many students can be guilty of plagiarism through lack of confidence in their ability to express themselves well.

> *I had previously been criticised for plagiarism [...] I find it very difficult to be selective in picking out what is really important. It's a case of adapting to computer-based learning, and knowing how to adapt.* (OU student)

Others turn to essay banks on the Internet because of poor time management, and the urgent need to produce written work to meet an impending deadline. The problem may be particularly acute for students who are not studying in their native tongue. Not only is the language unfamiliar, the academic protocol may be similarly opaque.

Whatever the student's motivation, the issue of plagiarism is of grave concern. There are sometimes telltale signs for the tutor; for example, you may notice that your student's writing is atypically fluent or perhaps that there are sudden changes in style. You might also see header or footer information from a website which has inadvertently been left on the script, or even sudden changes in the student's usual font or colour: some students can be astonishingly lax about cut and paste routines. There may also be sources which were not on your reading list, or perhaps sources which are out of date.

Some institutions now use automated plagiarism detection systems in which students submit their written work in electronic form to a detection facility. This compares their work against electronic sources and produces an originality report. Plagiarism can also be addressed through good practice, and Table 12.1 is a summary of some helpful recommendations.

Table 12.1   Plagiarism.   Summary   of   good   practice   recommendations (Reproduced with kind permission from Carroll and Appleton, 2001)

Lecturers and Teachers	Institutions
Rewrite/modify all assessment task, each time the course is taught	Invest time and energy into reaching consensus on defining breaches of academic regulations then disseminate them widely to academics and students
Consider the learning outcomes for the course and decrease those that ask for knowledge and understanding, substituting instead those that require analysis, evaluation and synthesis; consider adding information gathering to learning outcomes	Treat all instances of plagiarism formally with penalties and tariffs adjusted to fit student circumstances; inform students clearly of the policy, how they must comply and how they will be helped to do so
Design in assessment tasks with multiple solutions or artefacts	Design in compulsory teaching sessions on academic writing and citation skills where students can apply the skills to discipline-specific contents as part of their core assessment tasks
Integrate tasks so each builds on the other; design in checks that do not require teacher time but do require student effort. Be careful to only check, not assess, the intermediate tasks. Set a variety of assessment tasks, choosing those less likely to already exist	Create administrative and institutional systems to collect, record and return coursework securely
Ensure that students are taught how to avoid plagiarism with active learning techniques, providing opportunities for discussion, practice and feedback; this instruction works best integrated into discipline-specific contexts	Define clearly the respective roles of the examination board and the disciplinary procedure in cases of plagiarism, and any interrelation between them; ensure that all parties are aware of and adhere to their respective limits
Academic staff need to be seen to be adhering to the behaviours they ask of their students and taking steps to defend them from abuse	Make the disciplinary process a place where learning can occur as well as punishment
	Give the responsibility for dealing with all cases of plagiarism to a small number of staff in each subject area, who are properly trained and who will work as a team across the institution
	Establish 'fast-track' disciplinary procedures for dealing with minor and uncontested cases of plagiarism and clearly define the limits of their use
	Design a simple disciplinary record-keeping system that will enable you to monitor which plagiarism problems are occurring where, and how effective different strategies and initiatives are in addressing these problems

Carroll and Appleton suggest a variety of very helpful ways in which assessment design can discourage plagiarism. These include:

- Show students examples of good and bad practice, and then give them an opportunity to discuss the implications. Students might be referred to work on one of the many essay banks on the Internet, and asked to mark a couple of essays using agreed criteria.
- Include an exercise on paraphrasing: show students two paraphrased versions of the same text and encourage them to discuss the differences.
- Design assessment that requires students to compare concepts from course texts with experience or knowledge of current affairs.
- Ask for an outline, rather than a finished product: that makes it more difficult to cheat.
- Include a reflective component, such as 'What I learnt from writing this report' or 'How I would have done this differently, with hindsight'.

The first two of these ideas could readily be delivered using a network, or of course in a classroom if one is available. Here is an idea for using a computer conference for helping students to understand what paraphrasing is all about.

LEARNING TO PARAPHRASE

What do you understand by paraphrasing?
- Post a message to the conference explaining what you think that means.

(A few days later, a paragraph from a resource is posted to the conference.)
- Try to paraphrase this paragraph, and post your work to the conference.

(A few days later, two pieces of 'student work' based on the resource posted previously, are posted to the conference:
- a well paraphrased piece, which distinguishes quotes from argument, or makes appropriate use of diagrams from the text;
- a cut-and-paste piece with the odd word changed.)

- Read the two pieces of student work.
- Which do you think is good practice in paraphrasing? What are your reasons?

There are many other ways in which computer conferences may be used for delivering examples of appropriate writing, and I will discuss their use in the context of developing e-writers in the next chapter. You will see that there is considerable overlap between e-investigating and e-writing.

IN SUMMARY

Information literacy is a complex area which has become of particular relevance with the ready availability of web-based resources. Apart from familiarity with appropriate tools, there are generic skills for students to learn, but competence is also related to an understanding of the discipline and academic conventions as well as to the student's motivation and academic level. Helping students to be competent e-investigators may be achieved through a combination of:

- generic guides to appropriate use of search engines and the evaluation of resources; and
- activities embedded within the course: if face-to-face workshops are not feasible, then such activities need to be closely tied to the assessment.

RESOURCES

Candy, P. (2000) Mining in Ciberia. Researching information literacy for the digital age. In: C. Bruce and P. Candy (eds) *Information Literacy Around the World. Advances in Programmes and Research*. Centre for Information Studies, Charles Sturt University, Wagga Wagga, Occasional Publications No. 1.

Carroll, J. and Appleton, J. (2001) Plagiarism. A good practice guide. (JISC) http://www.jisc.ac.uk/uploaded_documents/brookes.pdf (accessed 29 July 2004).

Macdonald, J., Heap, N. and Mason, R. (2001) Have I learnt it? Evaluating skills for resource based study using electronic resources. *British Journal of Educational Technology* 32 (4), pp. 419–434.

McDowell, L. (2002) Electronic information resources in undergraduate education: an exploratory study of opportunities for student learning and independence. *British Journal of Educational Technology* 33(3), pp. 255–266.

SAFARI: Skills in Accessing, Finding And Reviewing Information; www.open.ac.uk/safari/ (accessed 30 September 2004).

Snavely, L. and Cooper, N. (1997) The information literacy debate. *Journal of Academic Librarianship* 23 (1), pp. 7–14.

CHAPTER 13

DEVELOPING E-WRITERS

The use of networked computers has changed the ways in which we write and provides new options and opportunities for constructing, editing and sharing written work. Since so much of online learning depends on communicating using text, it is critical that students learn to write appropriately. We know that students' fluency in writing develops with practice and feedback, alongside their growing understanding of the discipline. But the use of technologies does not automatically encourage students into effective approaches to writing, and they often need help in appropriate use of the technology to support their writing development.

The aim of this chapter is to introduce ways in which a networked computer can be used for academic writing and to suggest how you might help your students to write for your course, while making effective use of a networked computer.

WRITING TO UNDERSTAND: NOTE-TAKING

Writing about a course topic is one of the best ways of coming to an understanding of course concepts, and of linking information from the course with existing knowledge and experience from other areas. It can be one of the great benefits of taking notes from course materials. Unfortunately, note-taking is a practice in which many students lack proficiency, with the result that they do not make the best use of the readings available to them. And, sadly, although some technologies encourage a variety of new approaches to note-taking, many are not particularly beneficial to reflective learning. For example, by using a word processor, it is easy to 'cut and paste' mindlessly from original sources, leading to unintended plagiarism, as students struggle to make notes that are as coherent as the original document. In addition, your students may have invested in a variety of electronic tools for recording notes, such as an electronic pen, or digital recorder to record speech. Such technologies encourage the verbatim recording of information, rather than engaging the student in active thought.

The important consideration should be to help students to learn how to identify what is relevant to their needs, so that the process of note-taking helps and supports their learning. The passive absorption of facts is ineffective for learning: they need to learn how to make purposeful use of new information. The technology can and should be used in the service of this aim.

Having started this chapter rather pessimistically, it is time for some positive thinking. Once notes are in electronic form they can be readily amended, formatted or shared with other students. Indeed, if students are in touch with each other using email or an online discussion forum, then they can learn from each others' understanding of course material and benefit from a range of alternative perspectives. Such activity might take place in the 'running commentary' type of conference discussed in Chapter 6. The following exchange illustrates how this works in practice.

SHARING PERSPECTIVES ON COURSE MATERIAL USING A COMPUTER CONFERENCE

From: Donald McMillan
Subject: Technology

Not including the last decade, has technology ever been designed to have a positive effect on the environment? Can technology ever be designed so that it doesn't have any negative effects on the environment?

From: Eleanor Allding
Subject: Re: Technology

Well, technology itself is neither positive nor negative – it just 'is'. The 'positive or negative' arises from the use we make of it or put it to. As humans we sadly are all too happy to benefit, but have not yet accepted responsibility for our deeds when coming to facing up to the negative impacts, although the knowledge mostly is within our hands, greed tends to get in the way. Which underscores the call for responsible 'good governance' and to hold political, economic and financial actors to account; not to squander our common heritage but to husband responsibly.

Eleanor

From: Martin Graham
Subject: Re: Technology

Flint axes created by Stone Age people was new technology to them at that time. Their development probably led to the most up-to-date 2005 technological developments which will probably be considered antiques in 2205.

The production of flint axes would produce waste material, early pollution, or if used for drainage purposes for their agriculture, a form of recycling.

From: Niall Worster
Subject: Re: Technology

I see where you are coming from, but do you believe that the Stone Age people, then considered sustainability and realised that they were using a finite resource and, believing that future generations will also want to benefit from the advantages of flint, so they discovered metals, which were renewable!
Niall

Technology can also be used to enhance note-taking in various ways. For example, it is possible to:

- summarise notes in a table;
- cut and paste illustrations or graphs from electronic resources – if properly attributed, they can be useful to summarise concepts;
- build up a list of web links and references from course reading lists, for use in assignments as required;
- compile a glossary of unfamiliar terms as new terms and concepts are encountered;
- use particular fonts, or the highlighter tool, to mark notes of particular importance;
- archive messages of relevance from computer conferences; and
- use Microsoft Word's 'track changes' and 'comments' tools, for sharing ideas and comments.

To help students develop good habits, you could include an activity on note-taking as part of preparatory work for an assignment. Students may benefit from practice in reading purposefully, with the aim of looking for information to answer a particular question or to illustrate a point. They could be working together in a classroom or be exchanging their ideas using email to a 'critical friend', working within a limited time frame.

SHARING AN INTERPRETATION OF COURSE READING

Read and take notes on Chapter x, as preparation for an assignment on topic y. You are required to:
- identify and summarise two points most relevant to the assignment;
- explain why you think they are important;
- illustrate one point with an example from your own experience (or current events);
- email your notes to your critical friend by <date>;
- comment on one point which your critical friend found relevant, using the comments tool.

Submit your notes, and your friend's notes with your comments.

Electronic mind maps

As an alternative to word processed notes, mind maps can be helpful for constructing an understanding of course materials, particularly for students who like to work with visual representations, although not all students do work in this way. They can be useful for drawing together a subject, and illustrating the connections between related themes. In this context, mind maps might be used for taking notes, for recalling a subject area during revision or for structuring essays. Electronic mind maps can incorporate pictures and diagrams as well as text, and they can be readily amended, stored online and shared with fellow students. Software for mind mapping is available on the web. Be aware that familiarity with new tools is not acquired spontaneously, and your students will appreciate practice and encouragement and the time to get to grips with its operation. You might invite students to complete a mind map as part of a reading task and share it with fellow students, as preparation for a face-to-face tutorial.

USING ELECTRONIC MIND MAPPING AS NOTE-TAKING

Read Chapter x, and construct a mind map of the main concepts. Subdivide them as appropriate, and include links to examples from your own experience.

Either: email your mind map to your online group;

or: present your mind map at the next tutorial, explaining:
- why you chose those concepts
- your reasons for linking particular concepts
- the relevance of the examples.

You might wish to amend your mind map in the light of your fellow students' comments.

Of course, there is no reason why the construction of a mind map should not in itself be a group activity, completed either online or in a classroom. While the process of reaching consensus is very much easier and quicker in a synchronous than an asynchronous environment, your choice of medium will depend on the options available to you. This distance tutor used email to her group.

⠌ BRIGHT IDEAS...

I posted a mind map as an attachment for one block of the course. The mind map was blank apart from the title. Students were invited to add concepts, examples, studies and legislation from the block and return the mind map as an attachment. Each student added to the latest version of the map to compile a summary of the block.

Sixteen students read the map and about half of these contributed to the map. In future I would introduce this at an earlier stage of the course so students felt more confident about this method of working.

(Fiona Harkes, OU tutor)

WRITING ASSIGNMENTS

Word processing offers new approaches to writing and presenting assignments, and enhanced possibilities for the redrafting of scripts. By using cut and paste routines, it is possible to transfer a piece of writing from one context to the next. In fact, the ease with which notes in electronic form can be cut and pasted means that they can be used directly as the basis for an assignment. At the same time, students might need to learn what constitutes acceptable practice for your course.

Many people find that it helps to avoid 'writer's block' if they can get some writing done quickly, however rough and ready. Instead of laborious initial planning, they will produce a rough draft, which can be edited gradually until it becomes presentable. The stages of gathering information, planning how to use it and editing the written version are closely interlinked and form an iterative process. Word processing can mean that we plan less and draft more. But of course we are all different, and there is always plenty of variation in the degree to which individuals prefer to plan a structure before they start writing, allow a structure to emerge as the writing progresses or perhaps start to write the most familiar sections, leaving the tricky bits to emerge later. Some writers are naturally Beethovians, others are Mozartians, and I expect some are neither of these.

I make notes in a Word document then cut and paste bits across. I find it a very creative way of doing things. I like being able to make one para grow and another one shrink. You can't just stick something in the middle if you are working with paper copy. (OU student)

There are other ways in which using a computer changes the way we write. Once writing is in electronic form it can readily be shared by email, between student and tutor, or with fellow students. There is scope for collaborative working and peer review, and this is described further in the next chapter. At the same time plagiarism becomes easier than it has ever been before.

How might your students be helped to develop their abilities in e-writing their assignments? Many students already have basic word processing skills when they start college or university, but they can benefit from some understanding of how best to use those skills for preparing and writing assignments. In addition, students may appreciate a discussion on approaches to writing when using a word processor, or an opportunity to exchange thoughts and alternative approaches with peers. You could consider awarding a few marks in an early assignment for appropriate layout and presentation, perhaps laying emphasis on using fonts and margins to distinguish between the main points of argument and evidence, if that is relevant.

CORRECT PRESENTATION

Write an outline for a report on topic x.
- List the main headings and, for each heading, add two sentences to explain what the topic is about.
- Select two examples for each heading, drawing either on messages from the computer conference or entries from your reflective log.
- Take care to format your outline, so that you make a clear distinction between headings, explanations and examples. You may wish to use bold, or italic to distinguish between the different parts.

This process might be formalised in a process of iterative assignment development, so that the tutor gives formative feedback on the draft. The value of this to the student is that the feedback on the script can immediately be put to good use. The final assignment is simply graded – any formative comments having been given at an earlier stage.

As an alternative to word processed assignments, there are options for writing in hypertext and for presenting work as a series of web pages. It has many well documented advantages as a way of displaying the relationships between concepts, of exploiting multimedia or of allowing the exploration of topics in a non-linear way.

I think in a pictorial way, and I found this medium helped me to express myself. (OU student)

WRITING IN HYPERTEXT

Write the outline for a report on topic x.
- Start with four main headings.
- For one heading, construct a hyperlink to two or three related sub-headings.
- For each sub-heading, hyperlink to evidence from course resources or your own reflective log.

Before students can be expected to make imaginative use of hypertext, they need to be familiar with the tool. We learnt this lesson the hard way on a second-level Education course. Students were informed at the beginning of the course that they would be required to write in hypertext for their fifth assignment, using a custom-written hypermedia authoring tool called HyperNote, and that the course activities were designed to prepare them for this.

Despite this good advice and plenty of warning, it appeared that many students had either missed out the preparatory activities or otherwise assigned a low priority to them. In fact, many students had really only got to grips with the tool during completion of the assignment. Consequently, their assignments were disappointing because they had put all their effort into mastering the software, at the expense of discussion and analysis (Macdonald and Twining, 2002).

The most important point for me is that it was not until [assignment] 5 that I understood certain parts of HyperNote [the course hypertext software]. (OU student)

Learning to write appropriately

Many students need help in learning how to write appropriately for a particular discipline. Their experiences of writing, either from previous courses or from other life experiences, may be quite inappropriate for your course. They may have great difficulty in conceptualising exactly what you mean when you ask for a 'coherent argument' or a 'critical evaluation'. It is very likely that they will find the terms used in your assignment criteria similarly opaque, and any well-intentioned feedback which you give them may suffer a similar fate. They may even turn up to your tutorials looking for cues as to how you intend to mark their assignments, possibly a rather enlightened strategy.

I have not got a clue on the sort of answer required. Total confusion over this one. It looks like – well – define the universe and give three examples. (OU student)

I feel that attending tutorials to 'suss out' your tutor is vital in this course (and other courses), as I suspect various tutors, being human, have different interpretations of what is required by this course ... It pays dividends to get to know your tutor's views, and play to them. (OU student)

Although your advice and explanations can help, it is far easier for students to gain understanding if you are able to *show* them what you mean. One of the easiest ways of doing this is to provide them with examples of well written material in your subject field and to use that as the basis for a discussion. A networked environment can provide an ideal way of doing this, because it can offer students the time to read and reflect on the task and on the responses of their peers. Using the assessment criteria, they can comment on the sample scripts and develop their understanding of what your criteria mean in practice. When they have had a chance to do that, they can be shown model answers.

DISCUSSING APPROACHES TO WRITING

Read the assignment question and criteria, and then post a message to your online group:
   • what do the criteria mean to you?

(Several days later, two model answers are posted to the conference.)

Read the two model answers:
   • comment on them using the assignment criteria;
   • decide which one answers the question better and why;
   • share your reflections with the group.

We have found that the time when students most appreciate this kind of help is at the start of the course, at a stage where they are grappling with a new approach to writing and the requirements of the course assessment (and, probably, if we are honest, at a time when they are watching for cues as to where you, as the marker, are looking to award marks). If you really want to grab their attention, that is the time to do it (Macdonald, 2001).

When I was starting, I was going into it blind, and model answers were a help, like: 'Oh yeah, I know where I'm going wrong'. Later in the course you can just get on and do it ... (OU student)

☀ BRIGHT IDEAS...

Students were asked to send a message to the (plenary) conference once they had received their assignments back, saying one thing which seemed to be valued in academic writing. The ideas were pooled. Structure, relevance, flow, use of theorists, concepts and references were among the suggestions. The students were then asked to send their favourite paragraph to the conference. The excerpts were used to illustrate the qualities above, such as how to create a sense of a flowing argument in an essay.
(Fiona Harkes, OU tutor)

I always tell students the average marks achieved by the group on a particular assignment and often the highest and lowest marks achieved. However, I always lie; making the highest mark about two higher than the highest actually achieved and the lowest about two lower than actually achieved. That way, the high flyers aim higher and the struggling students are not too disappointed.
(Dave Horan, OU tutor)

Sometimes it can be very helpful for students to see writing produced by fellow students, particularly if you are able to draw on a range of styles. You might consider using an 'electronic scrapbook' of writing samples, drawn from excerpts of assignments written by students. It is a way of using student resources to illustrate your teaching points in a variety of ways. Such a scrapbook might be compiled after the first assignment submission, as formative feedback to the group. I tried this approach on a second-level Education course at the Open University (UK), using it as the basis for online discussion on interpretations of assignment wording or criteria. It could potentially offer some relief to the marker's workload, because instead of giving feedback to individual students it is given to the group.

The e-scrapbook can be archived and used in subsequent course presentations, where it might seed a discussion as part of assignment preparation, although it tends to lose some of its 'today relevance' if the scripts are not from recognisable students in the current cohort.

THE ELECTRONIC SCRAPBOOK

Message from tutor:

Every course has its own particular approach to writing, and this course is no exception. I have put together a few examples from your scripts to illustrate ways of writing. You can learn from one another! Remember that when planning the introduction to your essay you need to set the scene. 'Why' is a good question to ask yourself when you are planning an introduction. Then 'what' definitions ... And 'how' you are going to discuss the topic. These items don't have to come in a particular order.

See what you think of these three very different approaches:

1. 'I am going to look at the situated view of learning as explained in the E211 course and give examples of personal experiences that show the connections between the theory and the practice of this view of learning ... '

2. 'What is a "learning situation"? Although in this analysis I use terms such as "my personal learning situation" in order to situate my argument within the context of the course, the truth is my "situation" interacting with another student in FirstClass is not the same as my "situation" reading a course text or authoring hypermedia ...'

3. 'The screenshot above, taken from a FirstClass conference, shows some of the participants in this year's E211. Traditional approaches to learning might see us as a uniform group of learners, all ready and waiting to be filled with the same information in exactly the same way. A situated view of learning would, on the other hand, acknowledge us as individuals, each encountering a different learning situation as a result of our prior experiences and the unique personal context within which we are studying ...'

The problems experienced by students in learning how to write appropriately are magnified if they are studying in a second language and perhaps accustomed to a culture which is very different to that of the course authors. Goodfellow and Lea (2005) describe an 'eWrite site' which they have constructed in order to help overseas students who study on the MA in Open and Distance Learning at the Open University (UK). The site contains quizzes and activities, examples of typical feedback and student accounts of writing in the English language. They plan to integrate use of the site as assessment-framed activity.

PRACTISING FOR EXAM WRITING

If your course has a final exam, students may be particularly receptive to additional help with appropriate writing during the revision period. We have experimented with sharing old exam questions with students in a computer conference and, having given them the opportunity to attempt their own answers and share these with the group, we then produced an answer written by a previous student, as a way of illustrating a successful approach. This has been very popular with students, who are highly motivated to seek advice at this stage in the course, and it is cost-effective, as we have been able to provide formative support to classes of 60–100 students at one time (Macdonald, 2001).

Wow! I didn't think it could be that simple! 48 words. MUST stop babbling in the exam. (OU student)

I think this person comes from the 'write everything you know about' school of answering exam questions. They are wasting a lot of words and time putting in detail which would not gain any extra marks. I can see the time problem. (OU student)

PRACTISING FOR EXAM WRITING

Read the question and attempt your answer (or the plan of an answer).

(Several days later...)

Comment on the answer attached to this message, written by a student last year.
- Does the answer address the question?
- How much time/effort went into the answer?
- Was the time/effort appropriate for the marks available?
- How many marks would you award this answer?

(Several days later, upload the scriptmarker's comments and marks...)
- Read the scriptmarker's verdict and mark given.
- Share your thoughts and reflections with the group.

IN SUMMARY

Modern technology has changed our approaches to writing and offers new opportunities for drafting, sharing and presenting work. At the same time, students need to learn how to use the technology appropriately, so that it supports their learning. In this chapter I have discussed a number of strategies:

- a 'running commentary' computer conference can be used to share a developing understanding of course materials between students;
- web-based concept maps can be used for sharing a description of the relationships between topics;
- students need to practise their basic competence in using the tools, whether word processing or hypertext, before they can be expected to write creatively;
- students need to learn how to write appropriately for your course;

- computer conferences can be used as a way of discussing the language used in your course, whether that is in assessment criteria, your feedback or your expectations of what constitutes good written work;
- students particularly welcome this help at the start of a new course or in the period before an exam.

RESOURCES

Goodfellow, R. and Lea, M. (2005) Supporting writing for assessment in online learning. *Assessment & Evaluation in Higher Education* **30** (3), pp. 261–271.

Macdonald, J. (2001) Exploiting online interactivity to enhance assignment development and feedback in distance education. *Open Learning* **16** (2), pp. 179–189.

Macdonald, J. and Twining, P. (2002) Assessing activity-based learning for a networked course. *British Journal of Educational Technology* **33** (5), pp. 603–618.

CHAPTER 14

DEVELOPING E-COMMUNICATORS AND COLLABORATORS

Communicating online is increasingly familiar in everyday life, as email is commonly used in a wide variety of contexts, whether for keeping in touch with friends, arranging meetings, shopping or booking holidays. Similarly, text-based chat, whether via mobile phone or over the Internet, is widely used, particularly among the younger generation. However, the use of these technologies for learning may be less familiar. Furthermore, communicating with a group, including people you don't know, rather than with individuals you do know, may be rather daunting, particularly if there is a permanent record of the messages that you have sent and now regret. The aim of this chapter is to describe what is involved in communicating or collaborating online and to outline ways in which you might encourage your students to develop their skills and confidence.

WHAT IS INVOLVED IN ONLINE COMMUNICATION?

Salmon (2000) maintains that online learning involves a series of stages which include access and motivation, socialisation, information exchange, knowledge construction and development. Her model illustrates the interplay between competence and affective factors such as growing confidence, motivation and group dynamics. The bottom line is that students will be unlikely to be competent at learning in an online conference until they are comfortable both with the medium and the group.

There are other factors which come into play here. Much e-communication is related to what I have already discussed on e-writing, because it is largely a written medium. If students are to communicate effectively within an academic discipline, they need to become familiar with the language of a discipline and the way in which it is used in your course. Lea and Street

(1998) maintain that this familiarity with the discourse is a defining factor in students' abilities to read and write appropriately within a discipline. This means that students may be very anxious about expressing their ideas on a subject if they are not sure how to use the appropriate words. They can feel even worse if the group includes students who appear to be extremely competent. Students may also benefit from an understanding of the conventions and your expectations for messages posted to different types of conference. So, for example, messages to a course conference might be rather different in tone compared with messages to a chat conference.

Finally, if students are required to collaborate to undertake a common task, as opposed to making optional contributions to a conference, then they need to practise team-working and negotiation skills, group decision making and task management, just as they might for any groupwork in a classroom. Again, affective issues come into play. For example, a sense of group cohesion is important, as is the extent to which group members interact and trust each other. You are unlikely to get students to work effectively together unless they have arrived at some mutual understanding and familiarity with each other.

It follows that the whole issue of learning through online communication certainly requires practice and will take some time to develop. However, if your students have been familiar with online conferencing in a previous course, then you might have difficulty in holding them back.

STARTING OFF

One approach to helping students to develop as e-communicators is to offer some advice on good practice (for example, see the information in the box on page 156). However, in general most students will learn by doing, and their familiarity and confidence grow as they practice writing conference messages on course topics and reading or eventually responding to messages from others.

At the most basic level, and particularly in the early stages of the course, the award of a few marks for an introductory message or a response to a fellow student can encourage students to at least start using the online conference. This is often accompanied by some statement of expectations on participating in the course. Of course, we live in a changing world, and where students have already been using online conferences on previous courses, there may be no need for this strategy.

> *An introduction on effective participation in online discussions, including technical guidelines appears to be an important prerequisite for successful collaboration. As to the technical guidelines, basic information on how to log in, how to post messages, and how to reply was relevant and is presented as a test discussion. Further, explicit communication of information on participation rates, expectations with regard to the use of alternative sources and assessment criteria was necessary.* (13, Ghent Univ., Belgium)

> *But what seemed a burden five years ago, when the diploma was first introduced, may be an expectation nowadays. People's competence in this area, and degree of comfort has increased enormously. People see conferencing as an opportunity for ongoing networking with colleagues. You have to be continually reviewing how people feel about it.* (34, Open University, UK)

In any case, in the initial stages of a conference with a small group, most tutors will introduce icebreakers as a way of getting students to feel at ease in a new environment with unfamiliar fellow students, just as one might do in a face-to-face class with students who had not met each other. You will find some examples in Chapter 7.

ONLINE COLLABORATIVE LEARNING

The benefits to students of collaborative learning have long been recognised, and collaborative working is relatively easy to arrange if students can be grouped around tables in a classroom. If students cannot meet in a classroom, then there are various options for collaborating online using a computer conference, which can be rewarding for the students.

> *This is a superb way of working remotely... Having written comments rather than speaking to them in a meeting, you can't interpret the meeting differently. You have time to reflect before delivering a response.* (OU student)

> *Knowing that the five of us were actively contributing and shaping our thoughts and developing ideas gave me and I think the others in the group a great deal of support. Above all, I really enjoyed this aspect of the course because I felt I could contribute.* (OU student)

In a blended strategy there may be advantages in conducting part of the collaborative work in the classroom and part online. It is a case of making best use of the facilities available to you.

GOOD PRACTICE IN ONLINE CONFERENCING

1.   Communicate effectively. You may be confident at sending and receiving email, but working with an online group brings an added dimension. When you are talking to a group of colleagues face-to-face, you tend to adjust what you say and how you say it in response to what you already know about the group and to reactions which you receive from the group as you speak. These unseen cues are largely unavailable to you if you are communicating online, and it may be some time before you receive reactions from fellow students. It becomes very important to communicate effectively without being pompous or alienating. You may encounter messages from fellow students which leave you feeling inadequate, unable to respond or contribute. There is no substitute for learning by experience, but here are some tips:

- Share some information about yourself with your online group, so fellow students have some understanding of 'where you are coming from'.
- In the same way, learn what you can about your fellow students.
- In the case of unhelpful or aggressive messages from fellow students, contact the moderator. They can change the conference atmosphere more effectively than you can.

2. Manage the messages. Students commonly experience information overload when conferencing, with serious consequences for the time they spend online. The following suggestions may help:

- Log on to conferences regularly. That way you are never faced with an overwhelming number of messages to read.
- Be selective about the conferences you join. After an initial tour around the system, decide on your priorities and join only those conferences that look as if they will be most helpful to you.
- Resign from marginal conferences. Conferences often turn out rather differently from initial expectations. Sometimes they evolve in unexpected directions. If they are not essential to your study, cut them out.
- Read messages selectively. Once you have belonged to a conference for a few weeks, you get to know the participants, and you may find you can begin to identify the most useful messages for your needs.

3. Develop a questioning approach. Do not believe everything you read! You can see conferencing as a safe place to practise your arguments: it can provide an avenue for developing a questioning approach to study and for trying out opposing lines of thought on your fellow students. Be aware that other students will also be doing this.

4. Practise writing appropriately. Be aware of the ethos and culture of the conference you have joined. There are many different types of writing in online conferences, just as there are in everyday life. You would certainly use a different style of writing if you were writing a job application, a letter of condolence or an assignment for your course. In computer conferences there is also a variety of ways of writing, which reflects the type of conference where they appear.

So, for example, in a course conference you will have the opportunity to discuss issues raised in the course texts. This is a great opportunity to try your hand at writing using the language of the course. See it as practice for your assignment writing. On the other hand, messages in chat conferences will always be closer to the sort of exchange you might have over a cup of coffee.

Macdonald et al. (2003). Reproduced with kind permission of the Open University (UK)

If all your students are expected to participate in an online collaborative project rather than in optional discussion, then you need to consider ways of assessing them. Collaborative work can be daunting and frustrating for students when potential collaborators do not do so. However, although assignment marks can encourage participation, collaborative assessment of groupwork is really the ultimate test of mutual trust.

> *To be honest, I think we have a kind of schizophrenia about collaborative working: we like the sharing, the sense of pooling ideas and picking up ideas from others, but we are less sold on the idea of relying on others. The commitment required to work collaboratively is greater than as an individual, adding to the time demands which are already a problem for most students.* (OU student)

The following account is an overview of the processes of collaborative assessment, and I have shown how this could be achieved in a blended strategy.

Planning collaboration

The case studies of blended learning contain many examples of collaborative projects in which face-to-face or technology-mediated synchronous meetings formed an important part of the collaborative process. These meetings were crucial, not only for students to meet each other and form working groups, but also for brainstorming ideas, making decisions about procedure, and in establishing ground rules and timelines for cooperation. Some found that an initial meeting was sufficient, while others planned regular meetings throughout the collaborative project.

Where such meetings are not feasible, the initial planning process can take place asynchronously in a computer conference, supported by the assessment. There is a health warning to this: where online conferencing can provide much-valued flexibility in study routines, particularly for part-time or off-campus students, the fact that they must work with others can mean a loss in that flexibility.

> *Disadvantages? Guys like me! Being stuck with other people's timetables.* (OU student)

One practical way in which you can help students with this loss in flexibility is to establish when they are able to contribute over particular time periods, so that they can be grouped together according to their availability. In general, an acceptable group size for online collaborative work is four to six students.

The online debate will probably be procedural, that is, a record of agreements negotiated on who is to do what and when, all of which can be reflected in the assignment.

BUILDING SKILLS AND EXPERIENCE IN ONLINE COLLABORATION

Describe your group's strategy for collaboration:
- What time scale have you agreed?
- How will you deal with reluctant participants?
- Who will edit the final version?
- What is your personal assessment of the group strategy?

We evaluated this design with students on the Open University (UK) second-level course 'IT and Society'. The assignment had a positive impact on the outcome of collaboration in a later collaborative assignment: it clearly encouraged students to get organised as a group. The students learnt by their mistakes, and feedback from the tutor, and gained a first-hand understanding of the issues (Macdonald, 2003).

> We recognised from our earlier assignment that we lost a lot of time in the initial overhead associated with organising the task allocation, voting mechanism, etc., so we tackled this very early and got ahead. (OU student)

Assessing product or process

Traditionally, collaborative work is assessed by the end product, which could be a joint report, website or presentation. The collaborative product is submitted as a joint report, alternatively in a blended environment it may be possible to make a presentation in a classroom for formative peer feedback and summative assessment on content and presentation. This might be enhanced by asking for an individual evaluation of the product or some reflection on how it could have been done differently. However, one of the advantages of using online conferences in collaborative projects is that it becomes possible to assess the *process* of collaboration in terms of the extent and nature of the individual contribution. This is important, because members may contribute to the group effort in different ways. We know that a collaborative product may owe much to the initiative of one editor or coordinator in the group, and some members might be particularly good at facilitating input from more anxious or hesitant members. You probably have experience of watching the individuals within collaborative groups in a classroom: some students are actively engaged in the task, others are supportive of their peers, while some gaze out of the window. A computer conference offers the means to reward the contribution of the individual, because the transcript provides a record of any discussion, debate or other activity. It might also serve as source material for students' written work.

The contribution of group or individual endeavour can be adjusted by assigning marks to reflect their weight. McConnell offers the following options for collaborative assessment:

- *an element for individual learning, e.g. each person's performance used to arrive at an average mark, or other reward for the group;*
- *a cooperative incentive for group learning, where the group reward is based for example on a group product;*
- *an individualistic incentive for individual learning, where individuals are rewarded for individual performance, but within a cooperative working environment.* (McConnell, 2000, p. 18)

Online collaborative tasks

Beyond procedural discussion, online conferencing can be integrated in various ways into collaborative assessment. For example, the group might be asked to discuss a course topic, contributing examples of real-life situations to illustrate course concepts or drawing on additional resources. Students can be marked on their contribution to the online discussion, as recorded in the transcript of the discussion. The following example assesses the individual, although it reflects on the group effort.

ONLINE DISCUSSION

You are required to contribute to a discussion on topic x, in which you draw on your personal experiences, and illustrate with the content of some relevant web resources. You should:
- contribute at least three messages to the discussion;
- select a message from one of your fellow students, and reply to it: remember to do so sympathetically;
- within your messages contribute two relevant web resources to the group, and one personal experience.

Submit transcripts of three messages that demonstrate your contribution.

With respect to conferencing/debating in this assignment, we HAD to use the conference to discuss the various themes and issues. This was because it was an important and specific part of the assignment [...] Some of us spent quite a bit of time producing our messages to ensure they were of the right quality. (OU student)

An alternative approach, described by Wozniak and Silveira (2004) requires students to reflect on the quality of their messages.

REFLECTING ON THE QUALITY OF ONLINE MESSAGES

Nominate three key messages that demonstrate any of the following characteristics:
- timely posting that allows adequate group conferencing before deadlines;
- posting which helps to promote further interactions with other group members;
- posting which demonstrates their role in providing feedback to group members.

Justify your choice of characteristic, comment on the level of interactivity, based on Salmon's model, and reflect on how this exercise will affect your future participation.

Sometimes online debate can be rather repetitive, if students find themselves agreeing with the enthusiasts who posted messages early. The following suggestion provides a strategy for encouraging independent thought.

Individual start. In this setting, students are asked to post their opinion or solution to the case or problem presented in the discussion assignment individually before going into discussion. While the activities in the online discussion groups were adjusted throughout the years, this aspect remained an important constant. The first three days of each discussion, students are asked to post their own opinion. During these three days, the messages do not appear on the discussion forum. Afterwards, all messages become visible to all students, and the discussion can start. Students explicitly asked for this delay, as they otherwise feel tempted to follow the same track as other students. (12, Univ. Ghent, Belgium)

A common option in online collaborative study is to ask students to share their interpretation of reading academic papers. The following is taken from case study 7, University of Canterbury, New Zealand.

LITERATURE SURVEY AND PEER REVIEW

- Students are required to read one paper per week and summarise the main points in one or two paragraphs. They are to post the summary in the conference.
- Other students may come in and ask for clarifications about the paper. The student who did the summary acts as an expert and tries to clarify what the paper covers.
- After one month, students are asked to draw implications, taking the perspective of their respective position papers, from all the reviewers.

- Students then post their position paper outlines for critiques.

As a further refinement, students may be invited to adopt particular roles in the debate, whether as moderator, reporter, and so on. This gives them an opportunity to get first-hand experience of various aspects of online collaboration, and is of particular relevance where online pedagogy is the subject of the course.

> ... in the second phase of the course redesign, four different roles are distinguished: 'moderator', 'theoretician', 'summariser' and 'source searcher'. These roles are randomly assigned to 4 students in each group. At the start of every new discussion assignment, the roles are assigned to 4 other students within the same group. (12, Ghent Univ., Belgium)

In the following example, two students are assigned as critics and two as defenders.

AN ONLINE DEBATE

In groups of four:
- Two students are assigned as critics and two as defenders.
- Each posts a 500-word position statement, whether for the motion or against it.
- Each student must review all statements and enter at least four replies, including one to each side of the motion.
- Each student submits their position statement, and a summary of the debate, including four points made for the motion and four points against.

Students could be asked to write their assignment based on source material and experiences in online activities. Although they are given individual marks for their work, this again implicitly reflects on the collaborative process.

USING ONLINE DISCUSSION AS A RESOURCE

- Write a report on x, based on the issues debated in your online tutor group.
- Summarise the content of the discussion by drawing out four main points and illustrating your points with extracts from conference messages.
- Reflect on the experience of participating in online collaboration, including a consideration of the practicalities for yourself and your fellow students.

Beyond discussing a topic and seeking out resources, students could be engaged in a collaborative product, which can take a number of forms. In the following example, based on the Open University (UK)'s first-level course 'You, Your Computer and the Net', for which electronic submission is necessary, the collaborative product is a home page. Each student is responsible for producing a web page on a particular subject. As a group they need to decide who will do what, what style of web page to adopt and produce a home page with links to the individual contributions. Marks are awarded for the individual web pages and reflective commentary, but not the home page itself, so students are not penalised if it is not a success (Macdonald et al., 2002).

COLLABORATIVE WEB PAGE

Group collaboration to create a web channel. The group produces a home page providing links to individually produced web pages. They must decide who will cover which subjects for individual web pages and agree on a consistent style for all web pages.

Individual marks for:
- individual web page in HTML with links to a minimum of five relevant websites, a review of each site and table of contents; and
- their reflection on the effectiveness of groupwork and technical/design features of the home page.

Developing self- and peer review

One of the areas where collaborative working in computer conferences can be particularly helpful is in the review of scripts, so that students can learn to develop a critical approach to their writing. The asynchronous nature of the medium allows time for reflection and so is ideally suited for this activity. Self and peer review can be built as an interim stage into assignment submission, through which students can receive feedback from their peers and may have an opportunity to assess their own work before they hear from the tutor.

It was interesting to mark another person's work, not wanting to criticise too much, but still be strict in a fair way. It also gives insight into the way tutors think and mark scripts themselves. (OU student)

Many students appear to have difficulty in commenting constructively on a fellow student's work; indeed we have commonly seen vague comments from them such as 'That all looks very good'. They may need help in learning how to do this appropriately, including some discussion on the assignment criteria if they are to apply them consistently. You might find it helpful to give them a framework to work from.

SCAFFOLDING PEER REVIEW

- Does the script answer the question?
- To what extent does it meet the four assessment criteria?
- Can you follow the line of reasoning?
- Are the resources relevant?

McConnell (2000) describes a procedure for peer assessment, combined with the negotiation of criteria, which he has run with small classes of postgraduates. They meet synchronously in order to form sets before working asynchronously.

CRITERIA NEGOTIATION AND PEER ASSESSMENT

- Each participant offers suggestions on what they would like to do for their assignment. This is done in ... the computer conference ... Other participants and the tutor offer comment.
- Each person plans their assignment and writes it, at the same time:
- Criteria for assessment are mutually agreed, and we think through what's involved in assessing each other's work.
- Copies of papers are sent from one member to another, so that we all have copies to work from.
- We start the process of giving and receiving feedback ... Sometimes the writer of the paper begins a review of their work, mentioning those aspects which they see as being in need of clarification or modification, or talking about some of the learning issues that emerged for them in writing the paper. Sometimes the writer asks others to start the conversation about feedback. What exactly we focus on depends to some extent on the wishes of the writer and the interests of the other participants, including the tutor.
- We assess/mark each assignment (self/peer/tutor).

(McConnell, 2000, p. 152)

IN SUMMARY

Effective e-communicating and collaborating requires confidence and familiarity both with the group and the tool in addition to an ability to write appropriately for the discipline. This chapter describes a variety of approaches to supporting students:

- online collaborative tasks need to be integrated with assessment if all students are expected to participate;
- in a blended strategy, the planning of online collaboration can be effectively supported by face-to-face meetings;
- the use of online conferencing allows for the assessment of the process of collaboration and scope for assessing the contribution of individuals to the group effort;
- assessable collaborative activities might include input to an online debate, the contribution of resources or the support and encouragement of fellow students;
- the transcript of the discussion might serve as a resource for a written assignment;
- collaborative products might include a written report, a series of web pages or a presentation;
- there is scope for self and peer review and for the discussion of criteria.

RESOURCES

Lea, M. and Street, B. (1998) Student writing in Higher Education: an academic literacies approach. *Studies in Higher Education* **23** (2), pp. 157–172.

Macdonald, J. (2003) Assessing online collaborative learning: Process and product. *Computers and Education* **40** (4), pp. 377–391.

Macdonald, J., Gilmartin, K., Clark, W. and Rowney, I. (2003) *Using a Computer for Study*. Student Toolkit No. 10 (Open University, UK).

Macdonald, J., Weller, M.J. and Mason, R. (2002) Meeting the assessment demands of networked courses. *International Journal on E-Learning* **1** (1).

McConnell, D. (2000) *Implementing Computer-supported Cooperative Learning* (London, Kogan Page, second edition).

Salmon, G. (2000) *E-Moderating: The key to teaching and learning online* (London, Kogan Page).

Wozniak, H. and Silveira, S. (2004) Online discussions: promoting effective student-to-student interaction. ASCILITE 2004 Proceedings. http://www.ascilite.org.au/conferences/perth04/prog/asc04-procs-template (accessed 23 March 2005).

CHAPTER 15

STAFF DEVELOPMENT FOR BLENDED LEARNING

The effectiveness of a blended course will be greatly influenced by the skill, enthusiasm and availability of the staff who work on it. They will need staff development to be effective, unless they already possess the relevant experience. In this chapter, I discuss the perspectives of academic staff and how this affects the feasibility or appropriateness of staff development for tutoring a blended course. I go on to describe a range of strategies for providing staff development, including the use of online media and conferencing.

PRACTICAL CONSIDERATIONS FOR TUTORS

Staff who are required to tutor on blended courses face a variety of practical considerations. They could be working full-time or part-time. They might be based on campus or working partly or exclusively from home. They may need to adopt new facilitative approaches, while adapting to a need for flexibility in working hours and agreeing to reasonable response times for queries. They will certainly need regular access to a computer. The place where they work and their full-time or part-time status influence how readily they are able to accommodate these new working practices.

Those working from home may experience limitations imposed by sharing equipment with the rest of the family; fitting their tutoring work into odd time slots during the day; working with ageing equipment or less than optimal dial-up connections. Those working from the campus may have little problem with equipment, but may still be fitting their tutoring around many other work commitments, as this comment from the University of Lulea describes:

> *The most common difficulty for the participants of the distance training course is what*
> *to do with their teaching subject, to handle the production of the study guide and lack of*

knowledge of what it means being a distance teacher. They are both in the classroom in the same time as they are running a distance course. They have too little time for planning, preparing for and producing their DE course. (44, Univ. Lulea, Sweden)

The case studies from the blended learning survey illustrate the centrality of enthusiastic and well-trained tutors for a successful blended course.

Challenges: 1. Making the shift from face-to-face tutoring to online tutoring, in particular when tutoring is a part-time activity and tutors themselves are spread out throughout the Caribbean region. 2. Re-configuring the course coordinator–tutor relationship. What are the key elements of the course coordinator monitoring [the] role of the tutor? (28, Univ. West Indies, Trinidad & Tobago)

I would argue that strong student support systems are vital, this includes tutors with the appropriate experience/knowledge. This course has been delivered with a team of tutors and it was important that we were all in agreement with the support strategy. (11, Univ. Manchester, UK)

Recognition that student WebCT enquiries would be answered (swiftly!) and that someone was listening – they weren't just left dangling in the ether! (14, Univ. Gloucestershire, UK)

... staff enthusiasm and skill are key to success, I would ensure that staff engaging in the teaching in a VLE are enthusiastic about teaching in this environment and have the necessary skills to use the technology. Having provided a number of staff training sessions, poorly attended, I consider 'enthusiasm' to be a key component to success. (45, Oxford Brookes Univ., UK)

PRACTICAL CONSIDERATIONS FOR STAFF DEVELOPERS

The place where tutors work and their status as full-time or part-time staff will influence whether they can attend workshops on campus or meet colleagues for peer support. Their existing skills and drivers such as the importance attached to other activities, for example research, will influence their interest and motivation to undertake staff development.

For example, we know that part-time tutors who work at the Open University (UK) frequently have a variety of other work-related experiences they bring to the job. They might be working full-time in other institutions or perhaps have a portfolio career. It is likely that these varied backgrounds and motivations will influence tutors' needs for staff development in addition to their attitudes to drivers such as accreditation, job satisfaction or the enhanced ability to support students effectively (Tait, 2002). A similar argument applies to tutors who are working as full-time staff, although their backgrounds might not be so diverse.

PART-TIME COURSE TUTORS AND THEIR MOTIVATIONS

An early retired physicist is committed to her OU students, enjoys the mental stimulation of teaching and the flexibility of a role that allows her to visit relatives and take on occasional teaching in other universities.

A management consultant enjoys the stimulation of teaching with the OU and uses his work experience to develop examples for student learning. He also cultivates networks through both activities and appreciates the support of belonging to a community through being actively involved in (tutor) politics.

A young mother makes the short-term choice to integrate different part-time research and teaching contracts, despite the complex demands of working from home. She hopes that her workload will grow as her children become more independent.

A professional engineer uses his OU teaching to maintain some stability and connections with academic life, during difficult transitions between full-time employment and freelance consultancy.
(Tait, 2002, p. 158)

Learning takes place in a variety of ways, which have relevance to appropriate staff development. For instance, Eraut (2000) refers to three different types of learning which depend on the intention of the learner. He calls them implicit (learning which takes place almost unconsciously, taken for granted); reactive (learning in response to a recent need for information); and deliberative (learning when time is deliberately set aside for study). We all learn in all of these ways at one point or another, as one tutor wrote to me recently:

> There is one thing that I have learned over the years when working with computers, you don't wait until you have learned it all before you consider yourself ready! Sometimes you learn on a 'need to know' basis; sometimes you learn by actively finding out answers to questions you have; and sometimes you learn accidentally because you clicked on a button or somebody happened to be doing something that took your understanding forward. (OU tutor)

The upshot is that effective staff development has to come in many shapes and sizes if it is to meet a variety of needs. Most staff development is designed to provide opportunities for deliberative learning, but official course completion might not necessarily be an appropriate goal for all staff at all times. It could be important to plan for ways in which implicit learning can take place and also to consider the best way of providing for reactive learning.

Of course, tutor perspectives and needs are not the only factors to take into consideration when planning staff development. If the institution has quality assurance concerns, it may be important that all tutors undertake the relevant training. If accreditation is important, there is scope for offering flexibility in the way in which it can be achieved, and this is a useful approach to accommodating diversity over an extended time period. For example, while staff may gain credits by attending a formal course, they might alternatively assemble a portfolio to demonstrate that they have achieved the necessary learning objectives, whether from short courses, reading or through work experience.

APPROACHES TO STAFF DEVELOPMENT

A variety of approaches is currently in use for staff development. In this section, I outline the potential for each strategy and describe some examples of present practice. One of the problems with staff development is that it is very often a 'poor relation', when compared with all the other duties and responsibilities of professional or academic life. That often makes it difficult to engage the time and interest of staff who are not natural enthusiasts.

Workshops and seminars

Face-to-face workshops are the traditional approach to staff development and remain popular for those staff who are able to attend them. Not only do such occasions provide an opportunity for discussion with colleagues, they often provide hands-on support in use of relevant software. A recent study of innovative practice in the training of teachers in e-learning, sponsored by Cedefop (European Centre for Vocational Education and Training) illustrated how in many European institutions such workshops take place as part of a blended course, involving activities in the classroom in conjunction with online support and self study at a distance (Cedefop, 2004).

Resources

Resources on the use of distance technologies or pedagogic approaches can be important for reference when, for example, staff might wish to check up a particular procedure at the point of need, an example of 'reactive' learning. Other resources may include self-study activities, thus providing for 'deliberative' learning at a time when it is convenient. In this case, there is no expectation that staff will complete all material in the resource, but rather that they will select those aspects that are relevant to their current needs.

Printed resources may be useful for carrying around, however resources are increasingly available in web-based form, where they gain the advantage of multimedia, the potential to be interactive in some way or the increased accessibility to relevant information through a search engine.

> *Online support materials for staff and students in use of the VLE have been developed in 2003–4 and are now available to all users from their front page. These include step-by-step video clip scenarios which can be selected for each feature of the VLE.* (38, Univ. Paisley, UK)

Whatever their purpose, such resources can be available exclusively to staff within the institution or may have a wider readership. For example, an innovative inter-university programme funded by the Scottish Higher Education Funding Council from 1998–2001 included a number of staff development initiatives and resources associated with the use of broadband network facilities, which are available to the academic community as a whole (see www.scotcit.ac.uk). The programme included SeSDL (Scottish electronic staff development library), a collection of reusable granules on staff development in both text and multimedia, which might be combined to meet the needs of staff in different institutions. The contents can be browsed by topic and discipline, and a lesson builder tool allows users to create new staff development materials. SeSDL serves as a model for what can be achieved in this area, although input ceased with the end of funding to the project (Ritchie, 2002).

One of the problems in any provision of resources, whether printed or web-based, is that they do not necessarily arrive on the tutor's desktop at a time when they might be immediately useful or relevant. For resources to be useful, staff need to know that they exist and what they contain, as well as how to find them when they need to. It could be helpful to introduce resources to staff at regular intervals, whether in a face-to-face workshop or perhaps by drip-feeding extracts into a web-based alerting service. Of course, if resources are accessible by search engine, then it will be less important to know of the existence of particular information and becomes simply a case of searching for appropriate information at the point of need.

Courses

Courses represent a more formal opportunity for deliberative learning than resources. Courses normally have a fixed start and finish, a cohesive group of students, together with a moderator or leader to guide staff and provide direction and sometimes an assessment strategy or accreditation policy. In contrast to a resource, the learning objectives are set by the course designer, although staff may also have their own goals. A course can serve to motivate and provide opportunities for feedback and so it effectively complements the provision of resources. The course materials may subsequently serve as a staff development resource, since staff often wish to refer back to material later when it is relevant to the task in hand.

There is a wide variety of formal training courses for online tutors. Some courses are conducted entirely online, while others adopt a blended strategy. Courses vary widely in their learning objectives: the effective use of particular tools, the deployment of online pedagogy, the design of assessment, the management of online time and management of changing administrative practices. The appropriate choice will of course vary with the needs of the institution and the existing skills of its tutors. It is clear from a number of studies that regardless of the content, trainees particularly value the opportunity to discuss experiences with their peers, as well as gaining a first-hand experience of what it feels like to be an online student. There is also much to be learnt from an observation of the actions of the course moderator.

As an example of shorter course presentations, Pegler (2005) describes the Hot Topics series: an innovative use of learning objects for staff development at the Open University (UK). Small nuggets of material taken from one of the courses contributing to the MA in Open and Distance Learning were redeployed for this new context. The Topics contained text together with external links, self-study activities, optional discussion and some multimedia. The expectation was that participants would spend two hours a week on each topic over six weeks. There were high levels of satisfaction with Hot Topics, but the pilot was dogged by low participation rates, and over 40 per cent of participants had failed to access any of the learning objects after the first four weeks.

This question of non-participation is as much a characteristic of short online staff development courses as it is of other online courses. If the viability of the course depends on online participation, it is critical that staff do participate or their peers will be disadvantaged. Sometimes the increase in flexibility which asynchronous study implies is actually a disadvantage for both staff and developers, because it can be difficult to accommodate 'time sharing' activities in a busy schedule. For example, Forsyth describes some of the practical problems which they faced at Manchester Metropolitan University, UK, when offering online staff development as an alternative to face-to-face sessions.

> *It was clear ... that, faced with a large pile of assignments to mark, a research paper to write and a stream of emails from anxious students, not to mention routine administration, finding an extra flexible hour each week is not easy. People were only too well aware of the irony that it was sometimes easier to find a whole day for a face-to-face workshop.*
> (Forsyth, 2002, p. 255)

There are various ways in which this issue of participation can be addressed, and they relate to the comments I have already made in previous chapters on assessment-framed activity. It is also important to communicate your expectations in terms of how much of the course you expect participants to complete and the extent of their active participation. At the OU in Scotland, we have had some success in piloting a learning contract for our online course in moderation, in which participants are asked at the start to reflect on a strategy for their own time management over the three weeks of the course. They are also offered a completion certificate if they complete three out of five activities in each week. This strategy has increased participation and reduced the course drop-out rate, presumably because staff had been given a goal and an opportunity to plan ahead.

Mentors

Many institutions appoint mentors within faculties. Their responsibility is to champion the cause of online teaching and learning, while speaking the same 'language' as their peers in the faculty. Such a scheme has value in mediating between the theory of formal courses on pedagogy and the reality, since so often conditions in practice will be rather different to the theory. For example, McNaught (2002) describes the deployment of two learning and teaching mentors at each department at RMIT, Australia. These mentors were academic or teaching staff, who were 'bought out' for one day a week in order to carry out subject renewal and to contribute to staff development activity, including practical hands-on sessions. The mentors themselves received a week-long development programme.

Mentors may also be effective in an online context, and it can be relatively easy to arrange for new staff to 'peer over the shoulder' of those who have more experience. Indeed, Bowskill and Banks (2003) describe how they operated a mentoring session in which the inexperienced tutor joined an online chat session run by a more experienced tutor. The visitor then wrote a reflective account of the experience, which proved to be instructive for both parties.

Using online conferences for staff development

We know that tutoring can be professionally very isolating for tutors who work from home or for other reasons rarely have the opportunity to meet fellow staff. We have found that in the rare opportunities to meet together it can be difficult to stop them talking!

> *Tutors need tutors just as students need students. This remote business is just what it's name is, REMOTE.* (OU tutor)

In this context, online conferences can provide a valuable channel of communication. Their asynchronicity provides an ideal context to accommodate variations in working practices, time and distance, and helps to fill the long gaps between face-to-face meetings.

Our experiences on the SOLACE project, described in Chapters 2 and 3, illustrated to us how tutors can benefit from this exchange, especially with tutors from other disciplines:

> *I always find it very useful to have a chance to communicate with other committed tutors. Tutoring is a very isolated job.* (OU tutor)

Since the SOLACE tutors were required to keep a standardised log of their activities, they found that they were able to compare their experiences with others. They particularly appreciated the discussion of practical issues surrounding online conferencing or challenges of providing face-to-face tutorials. Although some participants were novices in the use of online media for tutor-mediated support, they clearly felt reassured by knowing that others were in a similar position and that the occasional negative experience of tutoring was often shared by colleagues. Those with more experience of using online media had useful expertise to share in this area.

Conferences may be used in various ways for keeping tutors in touch with each other. Where courses are supported by several tutors who are otherwise unable to meet face-to-face, conferences may be used in order to discuss issues associated with marking moderation and the interpretation of assessment criteria. Other conferences may serve as the tutors' running commentary on the course: highlighting areas where students have difficulty, exchanging ideas on useful web links to further resources or perhaps on materials which they use in tutorials. If membership of such groups is a central part of the tutor's job and they are expected to check the conference regularly, then it can be a central channel of communication from the course writer or administrator. However, optional arrangements may also function sporadically but effectively. In either case, the membership is a relatively stable group of people who are associated with a particular course or courses.

A tutors' conference is an invaluable source of support for tutors. Ideas for tutorials can be exchanged, with activity sheets and handouts added as attachments to messages, ambiguities in assignments can be discussed and there is usually someone from the course team moderating the conference who can clear up any unanswered questions. (OU tutor)

There is also scope for using conferences to provide a forum for staff to learn new techniques and successful approaches from each other. It is important that such a forum should be accessible and on the same desktop as email or any course-related conferences, so that staff regularly 'pass' it while on their way to other duties. The success of such a conference depends on serendipitous encounters. I see no advantage in placing staff development activity in a separate area, unless that is part of an accredited course. In fact I think it unlikely such a facility would be used at all. By the same token, it is important that any discussion is 'one click away' – most staff have little time for complicated procedures and easily lose interest (see Figure 15.1).

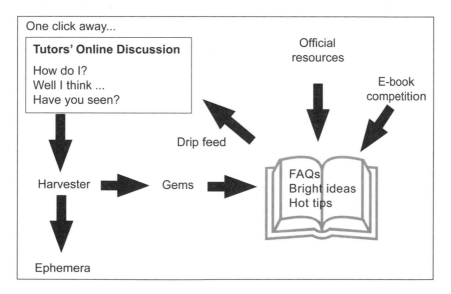

Figure 15.1   Informal networks for staff development

Over the last three years at the Open University in Scotland, we have run a successful conference for 200 tutors from all faculties to discuss approaches to supporting students using online media. The conference contains a central area for discussion or queries in addition to a variety of resources. Recent topics have included: the pros and cons of screen marking assignments; the introduction of new resources on tutoring; the use of broadband or dial-up at home; regular 'How do I ...?' queries; and notices of forthcoming meetings. The conference acts as a follow-up to face-to-face staff development workshops with some discussion after each event, but it also serves as a notice board and information point in a similar vein to the 'interactive resources' model I discussed in Chapter 6. We employ a moderator whose role is to respond to queries and maintain momentum in the conference, which ebbs and flows according to the topic under discussion and the work commitments of the participants. In some weeks there are no messages at all, while at other times there is a flurry of activity. We also employ a 'harvester', whose job is to archive any messages containing material to which tutors might wish to refer later into an archive of good practice.

As part of our initiative to encourage the sharing of tutor-generated ideas on good practice, we recently ran a competition in which we invited our tutors to submit short comments on how they use online media to support their students. You will have encountered some of their contributions in the 'Bright Ideas' sections throughout this book: some are extremely insightful, others are wacky, but they all bear the stamp of first-hand experience of tutoring. We maintain a small archive of these contributions on the tutors' conference, where they are available for reference alongside FAQs and official resources.

We believe there is much potential in providing a forum for the exchange of good practice in this way. Inevitably, for any resource of this kind to be sustainable, it must be easy to contribute to, easy to edit and easy to retrieve. Building on our experiences with this pilot e-book, we intend to investigate the potential of 'wikis' (web logs, to which anyone can contribute) as a platform for wider informal exchange among a larger group of tutors, using the existing entries to seed and encourage further contributions.

IN SUMMARY

The deployment of tutors to support students in a blended course involves a variety of adjustments to working practices which call for staff development. Such training might involve new approaches to facilitating more independent study, the appropriate use of asynchronous and synchronous tools, and effective time management. The content of the staff development and the approach used will need to take account of previous staff experience and motivations, as well as some consideration of the practicalities of supporting students using online media. I discussed a variety of initiatives:

- workshops and seminars continue to be popular for those who are able to attend and are frequently used as part of a blended strategy;
- mentors can champion the cause of online teaching and learning, while speaking the same 'language' as their peers in the faculty;
- the use of staff development resources is valuable, but in order to optimise their value, tutors need to know that they exist, how to find them and also what they contain;
- online or blended courses with a fixed start and finish, a cohesive group of students, a moderator to guide staff and provide direction, and an assessment strategy or accreditation policy can serve to motivate and provide opportunities for feedback;
- online networks can provide a platform for the informal exchange of good practice between tutors.

RESOURCES

Bowskill, N. and Banks, S. (2003) *Informal learning and mentoring amongst tutors in online courses: an action research study*. Paper presented at AltC, Sheffield.

Cedefop (2004) E-learning for teachers and trainers. http://www2.trainingvillage.gr/etv/bookshop/list.asp (accessed 18 May 2005).

Eraut, M. (2000) Non-formal learning, implicit learning and tacit knowledge in professional work. In Coffield, F. (ed.) *The Necessity of Informal Learning* (Bristol, The Policy Press).

Forsyth, R. (2002) Making professional development flexible: A case study. *Open Learning* **17** (3), pp. 251–258.

McNaught, C. (2002) Views on staff development for networked learning. In: Steeples, C. and Jones, C. (eds) *Networked Learning: Perspectives and issues* (London, Springer).

Pegler, C. (2005) Objects and issues – a Sunday supplement view of continuing professional development in higher education. *Open Learning* **20** (1), pp. 51–64.

Ritchie, J. (2002) *The Scotcit Programme. Achievements, Outcomes, Recommendations* (Edinburgh, Shefc).

Tait, J. (2002) From competence to excellence. A systems view of staff development for tutors at a distance. *Open Learning* **17** (2), pp. 153–166.

BLENDED LEARNING CASE STUDIES

Study No.	Institution	Country	Course(s)	Respondent	Email
1	Bergen University College	Norway	Medical Exercise Therapy	Aarskog, Reidar	reidar.aarskog@hib.no
2	University of Crete	Greece	Lifelong & Distance Learning and the Greek Diaspora	Anastasiades, Panagiotes	panas@edc.uoc.gr
3	Istituto Tecnico Agrario Statale Fratelli Agnosti (ITAS)	Italy	Basic climatology; English language module	Ardus, Jane	jardus@stevenson.ac.uk; fabi121@libero.it
4	University of Strathclyde	UK	Design, Manufacture & Engineering Management	Ball, Peter	p.d.ball@strath.ac.uk
5	Perth College, UHI MI	UK	Interpretation: Management & Practice	Bell, Helena / Nilsson, Tomas	helena.bell@perth.uhi.ac.uk
6	Oxford Brookes University	UK	Postgraduate Certificate in Teaching in Higher Education	Benfield, Greg	gdbenfield@brookes.ac.uk
7	University of Canterbury	New Zealand	Instructional Design and Technology	Chen, Victor	victor.chen@canterbury.ac.nz
8	UHI Millenium Institute	UK	Social Sciences	Cowan, John	J.Cowan@hw.ac.uk
9	Middlesex University	UK	Methodologies and Tools for the Engineering of Information Systems	Dafoulas, Georgios	g.dafoulas@mdx.ac.uk
10	Charles Sturt University, NSW	Australia	Web Based Information Systems	Dalgarno, Barney	bdalgarno@csu.edu.au

Study No.	Institution	Country	Course(s)	Respondent	Email
11	The University of Manchester	UK	e-Learning for Academics	David, Wendy	Wendy.David@ manchester.ac.uk
12	Ghent University	Belgium	Instructional Sciences	Valcke, Martin	Martin.Valcke@ UGent.be
13	Ghent University	Belgium	Internship in Paediatrics	Van Winckel, Myriam	Myriam. VanWinckel@ UGent.be
14	University of Gloucestershire	UK	Community Development Theory & Practice	Derounian, James	jderounian@glos. ac.uk
15	University of Leipzig	Germany	Media literacy – an introduction	Dommaschk, Anke	domma@uni-leipzig. de; stfrank@uni-leipzig.de
16	Liverpool Hope University College	UK	Innovation, ICT and Education	Donert, Karl	donertk@hope.ac.uk
17	Liverpool Hope University College	UK	Futurist Technologies	Donert, Karl	donertk@hope.ac.uk
18	Dublin Institute of Technology	Ireland	Learning and Teaching – online learning	Donnelly, Roisin	Roisin.Donnelly@ dit.ie
19	Suffolk College	UK	Introduction to the Internet	Funnell, Peter	peterfunnell@ suffolk.ac.uk
20	Suffolk College	UK	Supporting a Business Using the Internet	Funnell, Peter	peterfunnell@ suffolk.ac.uk
21	Suffolk College	UK	Supporting Employee Development through Mentoring	Funnell, Peter	peterfunnell@ suffolk.ac.uk
22	University of Greenwich	UK	Health and Social Care and the Information Age; Media Perspectives in Health and Social Care	Gill, Anne	a.gill@gre.ac.uk
23	Oxford Brookes University	UK	Education	Glenny, Georgina	goglenny@brookes. ac.uk
24	City University London	UK	Renal Care;	Hurst, Judith	j.a.bentall@city. ac.uk
25	De Montfort University	UK	Professional Issues in ICT; Computer Ethics	Jefferies, Pat	pjefferi@dmu.ac.uk

Study No.	Institution	Country	Course(s)	Respondent	Email
26	University of Glamorgan	UK	Enterprise	Jones, Paul	wpjones1@glam.ac.uk
27	Australian Lutheran College, Adelaide	Australia	Pastoral People	Kempe, Bob	bob.kempe@alc.edu.au
28	University of the West Indies	The Republic of Trinidad & Tobago	Various courses – BSc Management Studies	Kuboni, Olabisi	okuboni@dec.uwi.tt
29	University of Dundee	UK	Pre-registration nursing	Lee, Karen	k.e.lee@dundee.ac.uk
30	University of Dundee	UK	Post-registration nursing	Lee, Karen	k.e.lee@dundee.ac.uk
31	Foras Aiseanna Saothair	Ireland	Pneumatic Systems/Electrical Control/PLCs	Mooney, Michael	mmooney@iol.ie
32	Southern Cross University	Australia	Educational Information Technology (for pre-service teacher education students)	Phelps, Renata	rphelps@scu.edu.au
33	Bolton Institute of Higher Education	UK	Leisure Computing Technology; Internet Communications and Networks; Computer Games Software Development	Pickard, Poppy	p.pickard@bolton.ac.uk
34	Open University	UK	Management Studies	Power, Bronagh	b.m.power@open.ac.uk
35	University of Sussex	UK	Education	Pryor, John	j.b.pryor@sussex.ac.uk
36	City University London	UK	Higher Education – online tutoring	Quinsee, Susannah	S.Quinsee@city.ac.uk
37	Hainan Radio & TV University	China	English	Renner, Jean	jeanrenner@hotmail.com
38	University of Paisley	UK	Various courses	Rodaway, Paul	paul.rodaway@paisley.ac.uk
39	London South Bank University	UK	Geology & Geological Material	Sandford, Paul	sandfopa@lsbu.ac.uk

Study No.	Institution	Country	Course(s)	Respondent	Email
40	Griffith University	Australia	Adult and Vocational Education	Searle, Jean	J.Searle@griffith.edu.au
41	University of Sydney	Australia	Medicine and dentistry	Sefton, Ann	anns@gmp.usyd.edu.au
42	Aston University & Halmstad University	UK and Sweden	Various Courses	Smedley, Jo	j.k.smedley@aston.ac.uk
43	Vienna University of Economics and Business Administration	Austria	Tourism	Staudacher, Veronika	veronika.staudacher@wu-wien.ac.at
44	University of Lulea	Sweden	Distance Education – methodology and pedagogy	Sterner, Rigmor	rigmor.sterner@telia.com
45	Oxford Brookes University	UK	Health & Social Care Practice	Turner, Jill	jvturner@brookes.ac.uk
46	Open University, UK	UK	Learning in the Connected Economy	Weller, Martin	m.j.weller@open.ac.uk
47	INHOLLAND University and Universität Duisberg, Essen	Holland and Germany	International Communication Management	Westrik, Hanny	Hanny.Westrik@INHOLLAND.nl
48	University of Sydney	Australia	Applied Sciences (Orthoptics)	Wozniak, Helen	hwozniak@usyd.edu.au

BIBLIOGRAPHY

Ardus, J. and Fabi, F. (2003) 'A raga'. Scuola Online 2003: e-learning in a rural community: a tutor's view. http://www.sol.celleno.it/raga.htm (accessed 13 January 2005).

Biggs, J. (2003) *Teaching for Quality Learning at University* (Buckingham, SRHE/OUP, second edition).

Bowskill, N. and Banks, S. (2003) Informal learning and mentoring among tutors in online courses: an action research study. Paper presented at AltC, Sheffield.

Britain, S. (2004) A review of learning design: concept, specifications and tools. A report for the JISC E-learning Pedagogy Programme http://www.jisc.ac.uk/uploaded_documents/ACF1ABB.doc (accessed 23 May 2005).

Candy, P. (2000) Mining in Ciberia. Researching information literacy for the digital age. In: C. Bruce and P. Candy (eds) *Information Literacy Around the World. Advances in Programmes and Research.* Centre for Information Studies, Charles Sturt University, Wagga Wagga, Occasional Publications No. 1.

Candy, P. (2004) Linking thinking – self-directed learning in the Digital Age. http://www.dest.gov.au/research/publications/linking_thinking/exec_summary.htm (accessed 23 May 2005).

Carroll, J. and Appleton, J. (2001) Plagiarism. A good practice guide. (JISC) http://www.jisc.ac.uk/uploaded_documents/brookes.pdf (accessed 29 July 2004).

Cedefop (2004) E-learning for teachers and trainers. http://www2.trainingvillage.gr/etv/bookshop/list.asp (accessed 18 May 2005).

Collins, M. and Berge, Z. (1996) Facilitating interaction in computer-mediated online courses. http://www.emoderators.com/moderators/flcc.html (accessed 25 May 2005).

Collis, B. (1998) New didactics for university instruction: why and how?

Computers and Education **31**, pp. 373–393.

Danchak, M.M. and Huguet, M.P. (2004) Designing for the changing role of the instructor in blended learning. *IEEE Transactions on Professional Communication* **47** (3), pp. 200–210.

Derounian, J. (2003) LEAP (Learning Environments and Pedagogy) Case Study 11. Higher Education Academy. http://www.heacademy.ac.uk/Leap.htm (accessed 29 April 2005).

Donnelly, R. (2004) Investigating the effectiveness of teaching online learning in a problem based learning online environment. In Savin-Baden, M. and Wilkie, K. (eds) *Challenging Research into Problem Based Learning.* (Buckingham; OU Press).

Eraut, M. (2000) Non-formal learning, implicit learning and tacit knowledge in professional work. In Coffield, F. (ed.) *The Necessity of Informal Learning* (Bristol, The Policy Press).

Forsyth, R. (2002) Making professional development flexible: A case study. *Open Learning* **17** (3), pp. 251–258.

Garrison, D.R. and Anderson, T. (2003) *E-learning in the Twenty-first Century. A framework for research and practice* (London, Routledge Falmer).

Gaskell, A., George, J., Holland, L., Jordan, S., Simpson, O. and Spirit, J. (2003) *Supporting Students by Telephone*. Open Teaching Toolkit No. 20, Open University (UK).

Gaskell, A. and Mills, R. (2004) Supporting students by telephone: a technology for the future of student support? http://www.change.co.nz/docs/eden/Gaskell.pdf (accessed 8 October 2004).

Goodfellow, R. and Lea, M. (2005) Supporting writing for assessment in online learning. *Assessment and Evaluation in Higher Education* **30** (3), pp. 261–271.

Goodyear, P., Jones, C., Asensio, M., Hodgson, V. and Steeples, C. (2005) Networked learning in higher education: students' expectations and experiences. *Higher Education* **50** (3), pp. 473–508.

Harasim, L. (2000) Shift happens: online education as a new paradigm in learning. *The Internet and Higher Education* **3** (1–2), pp. 41–61.

Hartley, J. (1998) *Learning and Studying. A Research Perspective* (London, Routledge).

Laurillard, D. (2002) *Rethinking University Teaching. A conversational framework for the effective use of learning technologies* (London, Routledge, second edition).

Lea, M. and Street, B. (1998) Student writing in higher education: an academic literacies approach. *Studies in Higher Education* **23** (2), pp. 157–172.

Lefoe, G., Gunn, C., and Hedberg, J. (2002) Recommendations for teaching in a distributed learning environment: the students' perspective. *Australian Journal of Educational Technology* **18** (1), pp. 40–56.

Macdonald, J. (1999) *Appropriate assessment for resource based learning in networked environments* (unpublished PhD thesis, Open University, UK).

Macdonald, J. (2001) Exploiting online interactivity to enhance assignment development and feedback in distance education. *Open Learning* **16** (2), pp. 179–189.

Macdonald, J. (2003) Assessing online collaborative learning: process and product. *Computers and Education* **40** (4), pp. 377–391.

Macdonald, J., Gilmartin, K., Clark, W. and Rowney, I. (2003) *Using a Computer for Study*. Student Toolkit No. 10 (Open University, UK).

Macdonald, J., Heap, N. and Mason, R. (2001) Have I learnt it? Evaluating skills for resource based study using electronic resources. *British Journal of Educational Technology* **32** (4), pp. 419–434.

Macdonald, J. and McAteer, E. (2003) New approaches to supporting students: strategies for blended learning in distance and campus-based environments. *Journal of Educational Media* **28** (2–3), pp. 129–146.

Macdonald, J. and Twining, P. (2002) Assessing activity-based learning for a networked course. *British Journal of Educational Technology* **33** (5), pp. 603–618.

Macdonald, J., Warnecke, S., Barclay, F., Kilgore, J., Buckland, C. and McLeod, G. (2004) Comparing synchronous tuition in languages and maths/computing. A role for Lyceum. http://kn.open.ac.uk/document.cfm?documentid=5692 (accessed 2 June 2005).

Macdonald, J., Weller, M.J. and Mason, R. (2002) Meeting the assessment demands of networked courses. *International Journal on E-Learning* **1** (1).

Mason, R. (2002) *E-learning: what have we learnt? Improving student learning using learning technology* (Proceedings of the 2001 9th International Symposium), pp. 27–34.

McAteer, E., Tolmie, A., Crook, C. and McLeod, H. (2000) Learning networks: communication skills. Final report to the Joint Information Systems Committee; see www.gla.ac.uk/lncs (accessed 26 May 2005).

McConnell, D. (2000) *Implementing Computer-supported Cooperative Learning* (London, Kogan Page, second edition).

McDowell, L. (2002) Electronic information resources in undergraduate education: an exploratory study of opportunities for student learning and independence. *British Journal of Educational Technology* **33** (3), pp. 255–266.

McNaught, C. (2002) Views on staff development for networked learning.

In: Steeples, C. and Jones, C. (eds) *Networked Learning: Perspectives and issues* (London, Springer).

Miller, C., Jones, P., Packham, G. and Thomas, B. (2004) A viable solution: the case for blended delivery on an online learning programme. Proceedings of the 4th Networked Learning Conference, Sheffield.

Morgan, A. and Beaty, L. (1997) The world of the learner. In *The Experience of Learning*, ed. Marton, F., Hounsell, D. and Entwistle, N. (Edinburgh, Scottish Academic Press, second edition).

Morón-García, S. (2004) *Understanding lecturers' use of virtual learning environments to support face-to-face teaching in UK higher education* (unpublished doctoral thesis, Open University, UK).

Nicol, D.J. and Macfarlane-Dick, D. (2004). Rethinking formative assessment in HE: a theoretical model and seven principles of good feedback practice. http://www.heacademy.ac.uk/assessment/ASS051D_SENLEF_model. doc (accessed 22 May 2005).

Pegler, C. (2005) Objects and issues – a Sunday supplement view of continuing professional development in higher education. *Open Learning* **20** (1), pp. 51–64.

Perry, W.G. (1970) *Forms of Intellectual and Ethical Development in the College Years* (New York, Holt Rhinehart and Winston).

Ritchie, J. (2002) *The Scotcit Programme. Achievements, Outcomes, Recommendations* (Edinburgh, Shefc).

SAFARI: Skills in Accessing, Finding And Reviewing Information; www. open.ac.uk/safari/ (accessed 30 September 2004).

Salmon, G. (2000) *E-moderating: The key to teaching and learning online* (London, Kogan Page).

Salmon, G. (2002) *Etivities. The Key to Active Online Learning* (London, Kogan Page).

Simpson, O. (2000) *Supporting Students in Open and Distance Learning* (London, Kogan Page).

Snavely, L. and Cooper, N. (1997) The information literacy debate. *Journal of Academic Librarianship* **23** (1), pp. 7–14.

Tait, J. (2002) From competence to excellence. A systems view of staff development for tutors at a distance. *Open Learning* **17** (2), pp. 153–166.

Taylor, E., Morgan, A.R. and Gibbs, G. (1981) The orientations of Open University students to their studies. *Teaching at a Distance* **20**, pp. 3–12.

Wozniak, H. and Silveira, S. (2004) Online discussions: promoting effective student-to-student interaction. ASCILITE 2004 Proceedings. http://www. ascilite.org.au/conferences/perth04/prog/asc04-procs-template (accessed

23 March 2005).

Zhang, W. and Perris, K. (2004) Researching the efficacy of online learning: a collaborative effort amongst scholars in Asian open universities. *Open Learning* **19** (3), pp. 247–264.

INDEX

The Student Skills Guide
Second Edition
Sue Drew and Rosie Bingham

The Student Skills Guide first came out in 1997, and has since when it has become established as a leading Key Skills and study skills text, with adoptions throughout the country and overseas.

This new edition reflects the changes that have taken place in that time, in particular to the QCA Key Skills. It is now thoroughly updated as well as including a range of new chapters.

Structured, straightforward guidance is given on the following topics:

- Identifying Strengths and Improving Skills
- Organising Yourself and Your Time
- Note Taking
- Gathering and Using Information
- Critical Analysis - New Chapter!
- Essay Writing - New Chapters!
- Report Writing
- Oral Presentation
- Visual Communication - New Chapter!
- Solving Problems
- Seminars, Group Tutorials and Meetings - New Chapter!
- Negotiating and Assertiveness
- Coping with Pressure
- Revising and Examination Techniques
- Improving Your Learning - New Chapter!
- Reflecting on Your Experience - New Chapters!
- Action Planning - New Chapters!

Building on the strengths of the first edition the interactive style enables you to produce a tailor-made plan for each skill that is best suited to your way of working, yet incorporates the essential elements

October 2001   Paperback   0 566 08430 9   446 pages   £17.00

GOWER

Mastering University
Compiled by **Colin Beard,**
Sheffield Hallam University Enterprises Ltd.

This CD-ROM takes you through a journey into the world of learning.
Starting in the United Kingdom's first National Park, you will be taken into
the cafés of the University and into the lecture theatres.

You can imagine yourself alongside other students as they complete tasks
and discuss issues. You can navigate your way around by using the GPS
finder screen.

There are text files, video clips, tasks to complete and one-to-one tutorials
that will introduce models and concepts. They are all designed to help you
develop and master your learning skills: writing introductions, conclusions,
literature reviews and the development of critical and creative thinking, and
higher 'levels' of thought.

You will be asked to consider and understand issues such as where and
when you learn and what mental states you are in at the time, and you
will be shown a session called 'coffee and papers' where mood setting and
relaxation are important to learning. Watch the kite surfers too - it will help
you understand that studying is about highs and lows.

The art of Mastering University is what this CD-ROM is all about – try it!

CD ROM - Department Licence
November 2005   0 566 08708 1   **£49.50 + VAT**

CD ROM - Site Licence
November 2005   0 566 08710 3   **£250.00 + VAT**

GOWER

The Interviewer
Sheffield Hallam University Enterprises Ltd.

The personal interview is used by many organisations to select graduate recruits and placement students. But no university or college has the resources to offer every student repeated opportunities to practise their interview technique.

With this in mind, Sheffield Hallam University has developed this multimedia software to enable students to practise these important skills of self-presentation as realistically as possible, and at very low cost.

It also helps students who lack the confidence to perform in real or simulated interviews and who need some private space to develop their approach and their skills.

The software works by presenting you, the user, with a wide range of interview situations and a choice of interviewer. It then takes you through the chosen interview and videos your responses via a webcam. These can be reviewed and re-recorded as many times as required.

The Interviewer gives students:

- opportunities to practice their responses to real interview questions, as often as they like
- a non-threatening environment to develop their skills
- the opportunity to review and reflect upon their own performance
- additional feedback and guidance presented on screen or as printed handouts
- flexible use, either as a stand-alone resource or as part of a course or module on career planning.

CD ROM   **April 2004**   **0 566 08608 5**   **£250.00 + VAT**

GOWER

Join our e-mail newsletter

Gower is widely recognized as one of the world's leading publishers on management and business practice. Its programmes range from 1000-page handbooks through practical manuals to popular paperbacks. These cover all the main functions of management: human resource development, sales and marketing, project management, finance, and so on. Gower also produces training videos and activities manuals on a wide range of management skills.

As our list is constantly developing you may find it difficult to keep abreast of new titles. With this in mind we offer a free e-mail news service, approximately once every two months, which provides a brief overview of the most recent titles and links into our catalogue, should you wish to read more or see sample pages.

To sign up to this service, send your request via e-mail to info@gowerpub.com. Please put your e-mail address in the body of the e-mail as confirmation of your agreement to receive information in this way.

GOWER